Marketing:
A Primer for Business Executives

Marketing:
A Primer for Business Executives

Giri Dua, DBA
Chairman and Managing Director
Training & Advanced Studies in Management and Communications Ltd.
Pune, India

Donald Grunewald, DBA
Professor of Strategic Management
Hagan School of Business, Iona College
New Rochelle, New York, USA

NA

NorthAmerican

Business Press

Atlanta – Seattle – South Florida - Toronto

North American Business Press, Inc
Atlanta, Georgia
Seattle, Washington
South Florida
Toronto, Canada

Marketing: A Primer for Business Executives
ISBN: 978-0-9828434-3-7
© 2011 All Rights Reserved.

Cover art by Camp Pope Publishing.

Along with trade books for various business disciplines, the North American Business Press also publishes a variety of academic-peer reviewed journals.

Library of Congress Control Number 2011931621

Library of Congress
Cataloging in Publication Division
101 Independence Ave., SE
Washington, DC 20540-4320
Printed in theUnited States of America

First Edition: 978-0-9828434-3-7

CONTENTS

Introduction

The concept of marketing has been around since ancient times when persons would buy and sell animals such as sheep in what came to be called a market place. The modern English word "Marketing" was derived from the Latin word *mercatus* meaning to trade or traffic or buy and sell. Today marketing means much more than buying and selling something tangible such as an animal or a car or a house to live in. Marketing today includes concepts of marketing intangibles such as an executive marketing his possible services to a potential employer through an on line service such as Linked-In or a shoe merchant like Tony Hsieh, CEO of Zappos.com, "Marketing Happiness" through trying to satisfy a customer who wishes to purchase a pair of shoes or David Novak, CEO of Yum! Brands trying to satisfy a hungry person with a meal at a fast food restaurant like KFC or a politician trying to persuade voters to vote a certain way in an election or a museum director trying to market attendance at an exhibition of art to persons interested in fine arts.

Today almost everyone needs to know something about marketing no matter what his or her field of interest. The architect who has designed a plan for a new bridge over a river needs to be able to market this idea to some public authority that will fund the construction of a bridge. The inventor of a new way to reproduce documents must be able to market the idea to a company willing to possibly produce the new copier. The executive of an organization must be able to market his or her ideas to colleagues, investors and the board of directors as well as to customers deciding whether to buy products or services from the organization. Regulators and other government agencies must also be seen as customers and marketed to if government approval is needed for an organization to market its products and services to the public.

This book is designed as a short primer for the executive who wishes to learn something about marketing to be able to succeed in his or her organization. This book contains twelve chapters to help the executive succeed better by understanding the main concepts of marketing.

Giri Dua has had long experience in marketing with leading advertising agencies in India where he helped launch a number of well known consumer brands in India. He also has had long experience in education and training in marketing and other business subjects as CEO of a large educational training company. He has educated many persons in marketing and enabled them to have better futures as a result of learning from his experience and ideas.

Donald Grunewald served for twelve years as a college president where he learned that success for his college required not only marketing to prospective students and their families to help potential students decide to enroll at the college but also required marketing the college to government agencies, accrediting agencies and other evaluators of colleges like reporters who rated the quality of the college and that it was also necessary to market the college to prospective donors who could help fund the ideas of the faculty and others to offer a better education to students. He also learned while serving as the CEO of a museum and planetarium that the fine arts and astronomy are of interest to many persons but that the museum or other organization wishing to attract the public needs to use marketing to get interested persons to come to the museum to see the art exhibits or the shows on the planets offered at the planetarium.

The authors wish to thank the editorial and production staff at North American Business Press, Inc. who have supervised the production and editorial process for this book. This book has also benefited from the advice and encouragement of many persons. The authors take full responsibility for what has been written and for any errors. Special thanks go to the administration of both TASMAC and of Iona College for their support. Special thanks go to Judie Szuets for her help in typing and editing the manuscript and the index of this book in several drafts. Finally, we wish to thank our families for their encouragement and support.

This book is dedicated to our wives and children. It is also dedicated to all who work or aspire to work in marketing or use marketing in their work or other endeavors.

CHAPTER 1
The Marketing Concept and Buyer Behavior

Why does any commercial organization exist?
What is the prime purpose of doing business?

The answers to the above questions vary from person to person. They range from:

➤ to create employment
➤ to generate goodwill
➤ to utilize an individual's true potential fully
➤ to be creative
➤ to earn profits
➤ to offer service

The above list is by no means exhaustive. However, there are only two or three answers from the list above that come closest to the real purpose of a business activity. They are:

➤ to earn profits
➤ to offer service
➤ to create goodwill

If we closely examine the above three, it is obvious that "to earn profits" is of prime importance. If, and only if, the organization earns profits would any other goals of the organization and ambitions of individuals within the organization be achieved.

Let us now look at the above three backwards.

➤ *Who* will give us goodwill?
➤ *To whom* will the business offer service?
➤ *From whom* will the business generate profits?

Only one answer comes out loud and clear — **"the customer"**

Without the customer it is not possible to achieve any of the above. It is said that any business has three priorities:

1. The customer
2. The customer
3. The customer

1

The process of marketing ensures that a sufficient number of customers do business with the organization, continue doing business with it, and bring in more and more profits. Therefore, no matter what your job function is, so long as it contributes in some form or another to customer satisfaction, which could be subjective, by doing such a job you are contributing to the process of marketing. There is hardly any job in the organization that does not contribute to customer satisfaction. Thus, marketing is not the prerogative of the marketing department alone, but the entire organization and, therefore, individuals forming the organization are also part of the marketing process.

Let us try to illustrate. You are part of an organization that manufactures office stationery. Your function is that of a storekeeper. A customer places an order for a certain type of stationary with your organization's marketing department. How will the order get processed?

Customer _____	Marketing department _____	Finished goods stores _____
Production department _____	Raw materials stores _____	Purchase department _____
Supplier _____	Raw materials department ___	Production department _____
Finished goods stores _____	Marketing department _____	Customer _____

The finance department that is responsible for making timely payments to the suppliers, though not shown here, is also vital.

The above chain and the marketing function are obviously connected in the first two elements of the chain. But how do the rest contribute?

Finished goods stores

When the customer places an order with the marketing department, the marketing department inquires with finished goods stores or the finished goods inventory department to find out about the availability. If the material is available it can be dispatched to the customer immediately and the customer's need is satisfied. Thus, the timely action from the finished goods stores ensures customer satisfaction. Presuming the required material is not available, the finished goods stores will send the requisition to the production department.

Production department

The production department can quickly execute the order, provided necessary raw material is available, and contribute to customer satisfaction. If the material is not available it can give a requisition to the raw materials stores.

Raw materials stores

Depending upon the availability of the material, the raw materials stores or raw materials inventory department can either satisfy the requisition or request the purchase department to procure the material.

Purchase department and suppliers

The purchase department can procure the material from the suppliers in a reasonable amount of time and ensure that the production does not suffer.

Each department is contributing to the satisfaction of the customer. If, and only if, each department works having a focus on the satisfaction of the final customer will the organization achieve its ultimate goal of maximum profits.

Marketing as an activity defies definition. The word is used in many different ways and as an area it enjoys considerable jargon of its own. The scope is so broad that marketing is often mistaken for advertising and selling.

Marketing as a discipline has evolved over the years. During the initial stages of industrial revolution there were a few number of producers and a very large number of buyers. The buyers were dispersed and competition was low. The aim, therefore, was to increase the production to keep up with the demand. This is known as the *Production Era*.

During the *Production Era*, not only was the supply of commodities limited, the customer had limited choice. Therefore, the effort of the organization was to pursue efficiency in production and distribution to bridge the demand supply gap.

Once the organization maximized its production capabilities and the competition in the marketplace increased, a sales force was hired to sell the product. The emphasis was on selling whatever was produced with little or no regard to the customers' needs, tastes, preferences. Henry Ford, the *Father of Mass Production* in the automobile industry, is reported to have said, "Let the customer buy any color car, as long as it is black." This is known as the *Sales Era*.

Over a period of time, competition increased further and supply began to exceed demand. It became necessary to outsmart the competition by offering what the customer wanted rather than what the organization chose to offer. The emphasis shifted from *"We will sell what we make"* to *"We will make and sell what will sell."*

The marketing department was now created and involved itself in researching and assessing the needs of the customers, advising the management on design, price distribution, and promotion of the products. Though marketing departments participated in company decisions, it was still a subordinate department. This is known as the *Marketing Department Era*.

Presently, the role of marketing is recognized as central, and it receives treatment equal to the other departments in the organization. This is because competition is not only intense but is also sophisticated. This is known the *Marketing Company Era*.

MARKETING CONCEPT

The marketing concept is an integrated effort which is consumer oriented and also conforms to the goal-oriented philosophy of a firm. It is a process of defining, anticipating, and creating customer needs and wants and of organizing entire resources of the company to satisfy them at a profit to the company as well as to the consumer. Marketing is now seen as the underlying philosophy on which other decisions are made. The elements of the marketing concept are crucial to a company's ultimate success. It requires examination of market needs and not the production capabilities. Goods or services as a means to accomplish ends are not ends in themselves when the focus is integrated; all activities of the organization, such as production, finance, R&D, and inventory control are integrated. The important thing to remember here is that the marketing concept is only a guide; the organization must consider its strengths and weaknesses and balance its goals, customer needs, and resource capabilities after evaluating the impact of competition, government regulations, and other forces external to the firm.

As marketing stimulates demand, its basic task is to generate consumer enthusiasm. A major portion of the revenue earned goes to cover marketing costs. Clearer as it may seem now, this is still far from a complete picture. Marketing is a vital link between the organization and the customer. However, both have conflicting objectives. The customer wants optimum value for money whereas the organization wants maximum profits.

THE MARKET SEGMENTS

Though many companies rely on mass marketing and advertising, it has been found through research that each market is comprised of a number of segments, each segment representing a group of actual or potential customers that have same needs that can be satisfied with similar products. For instance, within the market for automobiles, there are those customers who want economy and therefore may choose a vehicle offering optimum fuel consumption. Then there will be those more concerned with comfort, and yet others who will purchase the vehicle for its power. This is true not only of consumer and consumer durable markets but also of industrial markets. Therefore, we see similar types of equipment having varying degrees of sophistication for each segment of the market. In each segment there will be diehard loyals as well as totally indifferent customers. Mass marketing may not address itself to every single customer and, therefore, each segment has to be tackled selectively to achieve maximum profits. The market segments have to be discovered and precisely defined. They cannot be invented. Their precise definition will determine the profits that the organization can realize. The important considerations in market segmentation are:

➤ Is it accessible?
➤ Is it measurable?
➤ Is it profitable enough?
➤ To what degree can the organization formulate effective programs to attract and service the customers in the segment?
➤ Do all consumers in the segment share the same need profile?
➤ Is the segment large enough to offer adequate opportunity?

Any organization has capital and labor as its major resources and production, finance, and marketing as its basic functions. Each function has different tasks and objectives, has different approaches towards money, and needs different types of individuals. It automatically follows that though all are working towards a common organizational objective, there is often internal conflict.

Department	Approach	Marketing Approach
R&D	Functional features Few models	Sales features Many models
Purchasing	Standard parts economy of sizes	Large lot sizes to avoid stock outs
Production	Long runs of few models, average Quality Control (QC)	Short runs of many models, tight Quality Control (QC)
Inventory	Economic stock levels	High stock levels
Finance	Rigid budgets and controlled spending Inward orientation Reliance on past	Flexible budgets and flexible spending Outward orientation Futuristic

THE MARKETING MIX

The offerings of a company to the market consist of four elements, otherwise known as the 4Ps of marketing: *Product, Price, Place,* and *Promotion*. The marketing mix is the mixture of controllable marketing variables used to pursue the sought-after level of sales.

Product

The product range otherwise identified by the consumer or by the organization for a particular market segment would be comprised of various cues to the customer including:

➤ Features
➤ Options
➤ Brand name
➤ Packaging
➤ Service
➤ Guarantee/warranty

Price

The element of price consists of the following:

➤ The list price
➤ Discounts offered
➤ Credit terms

Place

So that the customer can purchase and consume the product without much difficulty, it is important that the distribution channels should be efficient and cover the entire market. In short, the product must be made available to the customer at the least cost, in minimum time, at a place easily accessible to him or her.

Promotion

It is not sufficient to manufacture a product that has quality and utility as desired by the customer, satisfying the customer's own equation of value for money, and being available to the customers exactly where they expect it. It is necessary to make the customer aware of all the benefits that the product can offer and, if required, convince the customer to purchase and consume the product. This is done through advertising, publicity, sales promotion, and personal selling. An optimum mix of these 4Ps enables an organization to harmonize its objectives with those of the consumer.

Today, technology is not a prerogative of the chosen few, but rather a vigorous competition. This has led to more and more products and services being not only similar, but also made available at similar prices. Thus, the importance of the first two elements of the marketing mix — product and price — becomes no longer as important. The emphasis has shifted to product promotion, which is a means of communication with the market. Often it is the only differentiating element. To enhance effectiveness of its communication with the customer, present or potential, the organization may resort to any or all communication techniques listed below.

- Advertisement
- Promotion
- Personal selling
- Packaging
- Display
- Service

A judicious mix of these is created to form an image or a difference in perception or both by emphasizing real product differences and/or adding a little extra. The "extra" may not always be tangible but its being intangible does not make it any less real. A common product, such as a ballpoint pen, may be sold primarily on utility consideration, such as BIC ballpoint pens, or status considerations, such as Cross ballpoint pens.

As a matter of fact, a single factor is not decisive, but there are many interlinking ones that enhance the complexity of the process.

From individual to individual, the importance attached to various factors such as utility, price, color, availability, style, or utility as a status symbol would vary. This does not mean that marketing people can elect to exert their influence whenever and wherever they want. But the entire marketing system operates in an environment that exercises control on it through various factors, such as:

- total demand for the product or service
- availability of capital and area
- local and international competition
- availability of raw material
- government regulations
- availability of distribution channels

Obviously, competition is a restriction. The era of monopoly is long over. Monopolies still exist in infrastructural services provided by the government. More and more companies will enter the market with the same or similar products or services, thereby increasing the competition.

7

The question still remains however: What should we call competition? Is it the exact same or similar product or service? Or should a book that fills leisure time be called competition to other forms of entertainment, such as television, radio, video, or theatre?

In terms of similarity, as in case of courier services, it is easy to identify the competition. In the case of a book as competition to other forms of entertainment, it becomes more difficult to identify. Therefore, losing the same to competition may not always be easy to regain. Thus, we can try to define competition as any activity carried out by other individuals or organizations in the same or similar market, that directly affects achievement of organizational objectives.

The competition comes in various types:

➤ Same product/service
➤ Similar product/service
➤ Better product/service
➤ Substitute product/service
➤ Generic

Let us look at the concept of competition in more details.

What does competition do? Competition affects . . .

➤ quality
➤ service
➤ price
➤ packaging
➤ market segmentation
➤ strategy
➤ profits
➤ survival

As competition is detrimental to survival and affects practically every single aspect of business, is it really desirable?

Everybody agrees that the main beneficiary of competition is the customer. Does competition offer any benefits to the organization? The answer is both *Yes* and *No*. Using the competitive scenario in the market to the organization's benefits will entirely depend upon the way the organization chooses to look at the competition. If the organization makes an effort to be aware of competition, it can use the competitive nature of the marketplace to its own advantage in the following ways:

1. Product evolution
2. Efficient use of resources
3. Effective use of resources
4. Improvement in quality and service
5. Opportunity to create new markets
6. Better understanding of the customer
7. Opportunity to learn

Apart from the competition, other external factors also have an impact that is either *long-term* or *short-term*.

Fashions change, therefore customers' preferences change. The law changes and makes it easier or more difficult to enter new markets or start new ventures. Technology changes, making the existing commodity more or less redundant, or at least the utility diminishes. For example, the advent of satellite and cable television has had a tremendous impact on viewership numbers of network television, thus reducing the advertisement revenue for the television network companies.

The technology of faxes, and now e-mail, has made it extremely cheap and expeditious to transport written messages. The majority of the volume of work handled by courier companies is that of documentation. As both fax and e-mail need telephone networks to function, they have had a major impact on the courier and postal businesses in many areas of the world. If the telephone connections really become available, on-demand fax and e-mail will become much more popular and, therefore, will affect courier and postal businesses dramatically.

It is the combined effect of these factors that can cause a shift in the market. Inability to recognize, anticipate, and act on these changes can make the product or the service redundant. If the competition acts faster and more effectively, a company may not simply be left behind but will be run over.

It is possible to convert these problems into opportunities by:

➤ Keeping a close watch on changing demographic trends that help in developing a suitable product line.
➤ Changes in government rules and regulations that can be used to the company's benefit.
➤ Creating new business opportunities because of technological development.
➤ Reducing taxes, which, in turn, can affect price and therefore the demand for the product.

To ensure the achievement of goals and objectives of the company in the face of external factors, the marketing concept has to undertake various activities that start and end with the customer. The figure given on the next page illustrates the statement.

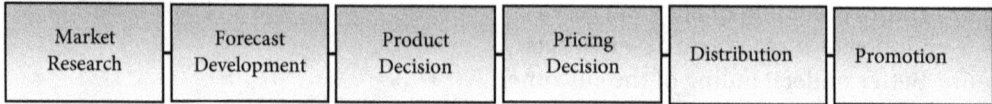

Market Research	Forecast Development	Product Decision	Pricing Decision	Distribution	Promotion

To begin with, market research attempts to identify and anticipate the needs and wants of the customer vis-à-vis *Product, Price,* and *Place*. To do so, it has to rely mainly on trends. The data so gathered is used to forecast intended sales and not to predict the future. This forecast also helps in forecasting purchases. Product development, though a continuous process, can sometimes be revolutionary or sometimes cosmetic. So long as the customer wants it and the organization can offer it, the development is desirable. Reaction to the price of a product can vary from individual to individual. Typically high price means better quality and vice versa. The pricing philosophy would also help in creating an appropriate image in the marketplace. With the product and the price in place, the company now has to look at the other 2Ps of the marketing mix, *Place* and *Promotion*. Though marketing intends to maintain a direct relationship with the customers, it is not feasible to do so. Therefore, the company operates through intermediaries such as wholesalers, distributors, dealers, retailers, and selling agents.

To make more and more people aware of the product and the company, various promotional measures are used. These include public relations, advertising, sales promotion, and personal selling. Though practically all forms of selling and buying involve personal interaction between buyer and seller (except in the case of mail order), by personal selling we mean companies or employees interacting with the end user. This form of promotion is followed mostly for industrial products. Consumer and consumer durable products are often sold through a chain of intermediaries, as explained earlier. Some products, though consumer durables, are sold not through a chain of intermediaries but through direct personal selling. The cycle, as illustrated on the following page, is ongoing.

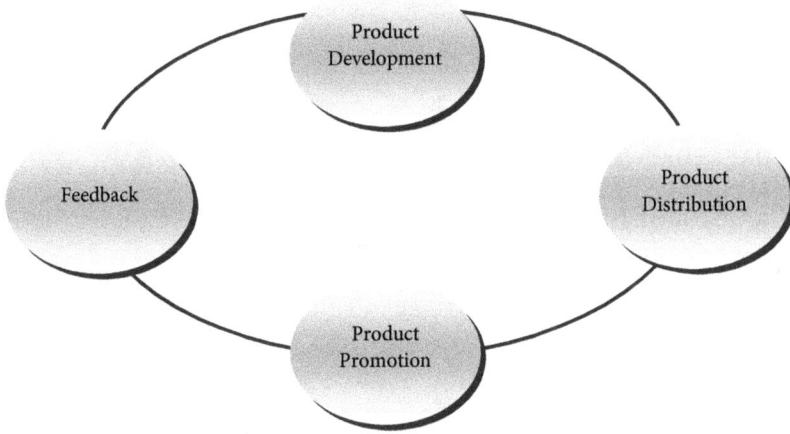

The activity of marketing, though exciting, is also risky. Marketing inputs determine the existence, function, and growth of the organization. It is not simply a departmental activity but is central in nature. To make any business viable, marketing has to create a situation and make the product or service available to the customer at the right price and at the right time. Unless and until the focus on *customer needs* is sharpened and the entire organization works towards translation of its resources into *customer satisfaction*, no organization, large or small, can hope to succeed.

CHAPTER 2
Market Segments

Though many companies rely on mass marketing and advertising, it has been found through research that each market consists of a number of segments, each segment representing a group of actual or potential customers that have the same needs that can be satisfied with similar products. For instance, within the market for automobiles there are those customers who want economy and so may choose a vehicle offering optimum fuel consumption. Then there will be those who will be more concerned with comfort, and yet others who will purchase the vehicle for its power. This is true not only of consumers and consumer durable markets but also for industrial markets. Therefore, we see similar types of equipment having varying degrees of sophistication for each segment of the market. In each segment there will be diehard loyals as well as totally indifferent customers. Mass marketing may not address itself to every single customer. Therefore, each segment has to be tackled selectively to achieve maximum profits.

Market segments have to be discovered and precisely defined. They cannot be invented. Their precise definition will determine the profits that the organization can realize. The important considerations in market segmentation are:

➤ Is it accessible?
➤ Is it measurable?
➤ Is it profitable enough?
➤ To what degree can the organization formulate effective programs to attract and service the customers in the segment?
➤ Do all consumers in the segment share the same need profile?
➤ Is the segment large enough to offer adequate opportunity?

METHODS OF MARKET SEGMENTATION

Markets can be segmented using several relevant bases. They can be based on the various characteristics of the customers, such as age, sex, education, etc. They can also be based on the geographical characteristics. The common methods of market segmentation are as follows:

➤ Geographic segmentation
➤ Demographic segmentation
➤ Psychographic segmentation
➤ Buyer behavior segmentation
➤ Volume segmentation

Segmentation based on region, continent, country, state, district, density of population, urban and rural characteristics, and climate of the area fall under *geographic segmentation*.

Segmentation based on age of the customer group, gender, family size, race, religion, community, language, occupation, educational level, social level, and income level come under *demographic segmentation*.

Variables including personality types, lifestyles, and value systems form the basis of *psychographic segmentation*. Psychographic segmentation facilitates the selection of people who en masse react in a particular manner to a particular emotional appeal and share common behavioral patterns as buyers.

Where the *buying behavior* predominantly depends on personality traits and lifestyle patterns, this method of segmentation will be useful. By this method, the consumers can be classified into several broad types: "playboys" and "stable citizens," "conservatives" and "liberals," 'leader" and "followers," etc. Buyer behavior segmentation is similar to but slightly different from psychographic segmentation. The primary idea in buyer behavior segmentation is that different customer groups expect different benefits from the same product and, as such, their motivations in owning it and their behavior in buying it will be different.

In *volume segmentation*, the quantity of the purchase or the potential quantity of purchase is the basis for segmentation. There may be bulk buyers and small-scale buyers, regular buyers and one-time buyers. They have to be treated differently.

Segmentation using several bases is possible

It is not as though a given market can be segmented only in one of the ways mentioned above. Customer characteristics usually involve a large number of variables. Therefore, a market can be segmented through a succession of bases chosen from the broad categories mentioned above. For example, a given market can be segmented using the geographical base in the first instance, followed by the psychographical base or buyer behavior base. In fact, the aim should be to go as deeply as possible in segmenting the marketing so that the most attractive and relevant segments suited for the given product and the given company can be chosen out of the total market.

THE STEPS INVOLVED IN
THE SEGMENTATION PROCESS

Whatever parameter(s) a firm decides to segment its market is based on, the task is an exacting one. Mere identification of a difference between one customer group and another does not complete market segmentation. In fact, the identification of difference is just the starting point of the whole process. Many other steps have to be carried out for completing the exercise.

The main steps involved in the process are as follows:

1. Assess the differences between one customer group and the other in terms of their needs and their likely responses to the product and other marketing inputs of the firm.
2. Find out by what descriptive factors or characteristics consumers of a particular type or disposition can be tagged to a specified segment.
3. Based on (1) and (2) above, disaggregate the consumers into suitable segments.
4. Analyze and establish whether it is desirable and possible to formulate separate marketing programs and marketing mixes for the different segments.
5. Find out which segments would be happy with the offerings of the firm and could, therefore, be considered as the natural targets of the firm.
6. Estimate the likely levels of purchase by each of the segments, especially the significant and relevant ones.
7. Select those segments that offer higher potential and that would be amenable to the offerings of the firm.

CHAPTER 3
Marketing Planning

We saw in the marketing concept that the activity of marketing is not the activity of the marketing department alone but all the departments in the organization work in a coordinated manner to achieve customer satisfaction.

Planning is the most important function of the manager, and *Marketing Planning* is the beginning of the activities for an enterprise. However, we cannot afford to look at *Marketing Planning* in isolation, as if it is the planning of the marketing department, but it has to be synonymous with overall business planning.

Planning bridges the gap from where we are to where we want to go. It makes it possible for things to occur that would not otherwise happen. Although we can seldom predict the exact future, and though factors beyond our control may interfere with the best-laid plans, unless we plan, we are leaving events to chance. Planning is an intellectually demanding process; it requires that we consciously determine courses of action and base our decisions on purpose, knowledge, and considered estimates.

We can highlight the essential nature of planning by examining its four major aspects:

➤ its contribution to purpose and objectives
➤ its primacy among the manager's tasks
➤ its pervasiveness, and
➤ the efficiency of resulting plans

The purpose of every plan and all its supporting plans is to contribute to the accomplishment of enterprise purpose and objectives. This principle derives from the nature of organized enterprise, which exists for the accomplishment of group purpose through deliberate cooperation.

Marketing Planning seeks to achieve the desired marketing objectives of the firm with the optimum blend of the available resources. It is essentially a set of decisions taken "now" on what must be done in the "future." It spells out how the resources must be deployed so that the set goals can be achieved.

Marketing Planning provides the necessary bridge between the organization and its customers, hence it should be rooted firmly in consumer satisfaction. It is the consumer who provides the starting point of all activities of an enterprise. The success of all the efforts of the organization will depend upon the quality of marketing plans that are put together after considering the environment, its perception by the management, vision, foresight, and so on.

PROCESS OF PLANNING

Being Aware of Opportunity	Comparing Alternatives in Light of Goals Sought
In light of: ➤ The Market ➤ Competition ➤ What customers want ➤ Our strengths ➤ Our weaknesses	Which alternative will give us the best chance of meeting our goals at the lowest cost and highest profit?
Setting Objectives or Goals	Choosing an Alternative
Where we want to be and what we want to accomplish and when	Selecting the course of action we will pursue
Considering Planning Premises	Formulating Supporting Plans
In what environment — internal or external — will our plans operate?	Such as plans to: ➤ Buy equipment ➤ Buy materials ➤ Hire and train workers ➤ Develop a new product
Identifying Alternatives	"Numberizing" Plans by Making Budgets
What are the most promising alternatives to accomplishing our objectives?	Develop such budgets as: ➤ Volume and price of sales ➤ Operating expenses necessary for plans ➤ Expenditures for capital equipment

Although we present the steps in planning here in connection with major programs, such as the acquisition of a plant or a fleet of jets or the development of a product, managers would follow essentially the same steps in any thorough planning. As minor plans are usually simpler, certain steps are more easily accomplished, but the practical steps we list below are of general application. These steps are diagrammed although it precedes actual planning and is therefore not strictly a part of the planning process — being aware of an opportunity is

18

the real starting point for planning. We should take a preliminary look at possible future opportunities and see them clearly and completely, know where we stand in light of our strengths and weaknesses, understand what problems we wish to solve and why, and know what we expect to gain. Our setting realistic objectives depends on this awareness. Planning requires realistic diagnosis of the opportunity situation.

In planning a major program, the second step is to establish objectives for the entire enterprise and then for each subordinate work unit. Objectives specify the expected results and indicate the end points of what is to be done, where the primary emphasis is to be placed, and what is to be accomplished by the network of strategies, policies, procedures, rules, budgets, and programs.

Enterprise objectives give direction to the major plans which, when reflecting these objectives, define the objective of every major department. Major department objectives, in turn, control the objectives of subordinate departments, and so on down the line. The objectives of lesser departments will be better framed, however, if subdivision managers understand the overall enterprise objectives and the implied derivative goals, and if they are given an opportunity to contribute their ideas to setting their own goals and those of the enterprise. A third logical step in planning is to establish, circulate, and obtain agreement to utilize critical planning premises. Planning premises are forecasts, applicable basic policies, and existing company plans. They are assumptions about the environment in which the plan is to be carried out. It is important for all the managers involved in planning to agree on the premises. In fact, one of the major principles of planning is this — the more thoroughly individuals charged with planning understand and agree to utilize consistent planning premises, the more coordinated enterprise planning will be.

Forecasting is important in premising:

➤ What kind of markets will there be?
➤ What volume of sales?
➤ What prices?
➤ What products?
➤ What technical developments?
➤ What costs?
➤ What wage rates?
➤ What tax rates and policies?
➤ What new plants?
➤ What policies with respect to dividends?
➤ IIow will expansion be financed?
➤ What political or social environment?
➤ What are the long-term trends?

The fourth step in planning is to search for and examine alternative courses of action, especially those not immediately apparent. There is seldom a plan for which reasonable alternatives do not exist, and quite often an alternative that is not obvious proves to be the best.

The more common problem is not finding alternatives, but reducing the number of alternatives so that the most promising may be analyzed. Even with mathematical techniques and the computer, there is a limit to the number of alternatives that can be thoroughly examined. The planner must usually make a preliminary examination to discover the most fruitful possibilities.

Having sought out alternative courses and examined their strong and weak points, we must next evaluate them by assessing them in light of premises and goals. One course may appear to be the most profitable but require a large cash outlay and a slow payback; another may look less profitable but involve less risk; still another may better suit the company's long-range objectives.

If the objective were to maximize immediate profits in a certain business, if the future were not uncertain, if cash position and capital availability were not worrisome, and if most factors could be reduced to definite data, this evaluation would be relatively easy. But planners typically encounter many uncertainties, problems of capital shortage and various intangible factors, and so evaluation is usually very difficult, even with relatively simple problems. A company may wish to enter a new product line primarily for purposes of prestige, and the forecast may show a financial loss, but the question is still open as to whether the loss is worth the gain in prestige.

Because there are so many alternative courses in most situations and there are numerous variables and limitations to be considered, evaluation can be exceedingly difficult. As a result of these complexities, the newer methodologies and applications of operations research and analysis are helpful. Indeed, it is at this step in the planning process that operations research and mathematical and computing techniques have their primary application to the field of management.

This is the point at which the plan is adopted — the real point of decision making. Occasionally an analysis and evaluation of alternative courses will disclose that two or more are advisable, and the manager may decide to follow several courses rather than the one best course.

At the point at which a decision is made, planning is seldom complete, and a seventh step is indicated. There are, almost invariably, derivative plans required to support the basic plan. When an airline decided to acquire a fleet of new planes, this decision was the signal for the development of a host of derivative plans — for the hiring and training of various types of personnel, the acquisition and positioning of spare parts, the development of maintenance facilities, scheduling, advertising, financing, and insurance.

After decisions are made and plans are set, the final step to give them meaning, as was indicated in the discussion of types of plans, is to numberize them by converting them to budgets. The overall budgets of an enterprise represent the sum total of income and expenses, with resultant profit or surplus, and budgets of major balance sheet items such as cash and capital expenditures. Each department program of a business or other enterprise can have its own budgets, usually of expenses and capital expenditures, which tie into the overall budget.

If done well, budgets become a means of adding together the various plans as well as important standards against which planning progress can be measured.

STRATEGIES

For a business enterprise (and, with some modification, for other kinds of organizations as well), the major strategies that give an overall direction to operations are likely to be in the following areas.

New or changed products and services

A business exists to furnish products or services. In a very real sense, profits are merely a measure — although an important one — of how well a company serves its customers.

Marketing

Marketing strategies are designed to guide managers in getting products or services to customers and encouraging customers to buy.

Growth

Growth strategies give answers to such questions as how much growth should occur, how fast, where, and how it should occur.

Finance

Every business enterprise, and for that matter, any non-business enterprise, must have a clear strategy for financing its operations. There are various ways of doing this and usually there are many serious limitations.

Organization

Organizational strategy has to do with the type of organizational pattern an enterprise will use. It answers such practical questions as how centralized or decentralized decision making authority should be, what kinds of departmental patterns are most suitable, whether to develop integrated divisions with profit responsibility, whether to use matrix organization structures, and how to design staff positions. Naturally, organization structures furnish the system of roles and role relationships that help people to accomplish objectives.

Personnel

There can be many major strategies in the area of human resources and relationships. They deal with such topics as union relations, compensation, selection, hiring, training, and appraisal, as well as with special areas such as job enrichment.

Public relations

Strategies in this area can hardly be independent but must support other major strategies and efforts. They must also be designed with regard for the company's type of business, its closeness to the public, and its susceptibility to regulation by government agencies.

To develop strategies in any area, we must ask the right questions. While no set of strategies can be formulated that will fit all organizations and situations, certain key questions will help any company to discover what its strategies should be.

To show how the right question can lead to answers, we will raise some key questions in only two major strategic areas: new products and services and marketing. With little thought, you can devise key questions for other major strategic areas.

New products or services, more than any other single factor, determine what an enterprise is or will be. The key questions in this area can be summarized as follows:

➤ What is our business?
➤ Who are our customers?
➤ What do our customers want?
➤ How much will our customers buy and at what price?
➤ Do we wish to be a product leader?
➤ Do we wish to develop our own new products?
➤ What advantages do we have in serving customer needs?
➤ How should we respond to existing and potential competition?
➤ How far can we go in serving customer needs?
➤ What profits can we expect?
➤ What basic form should our strategy take?

22

Marketing strategies are closely related to product strategies; they must be inter-related and mutually supportive. As a matter of fact, Peter Drucker regards the two basic business functions as innovation (for example, the creation of new goods or services) and marketing. A business can scarcely survive without at least one of these functions and will preferably have both. A company can succeed by copying products, but it can hardly succeed without effective marketing. And, as the world has grown increasingly competitive, marketing has become the tail that wags the company dog.

The key questions that serve as guides for establishing a marketing strategy are:

➤ Where are our customers and why do they buy?
➤ How do our customers buy?
➤ How is it best for us to sell?
➤ Do we have something to offer that competitors do not?
➤ Do we wish to take legal steps to discourage competition?
➤ Do we need, and can we supply, supporting services?
➤ What is the best pricing strategy and policy for our operation?

A TOOL FOR ALLOCATING RESOURCES: THE PORTFOLIO MATRIX

Strategists have been aided by a number of tools that help them decide how to allocate resources. We will focus on one such tool, the *Business Portfolio Matrix*, which was developed by the Boston Consulting Group (BCG).

The following diagram is a simplified version of the matrix and shows the link-ages between the growth rate of the business and the relative competitive position of the firm, identified by the market share. Businesses in the "question mark" quadrant — sometimes called the "problem child" quadrant — with a

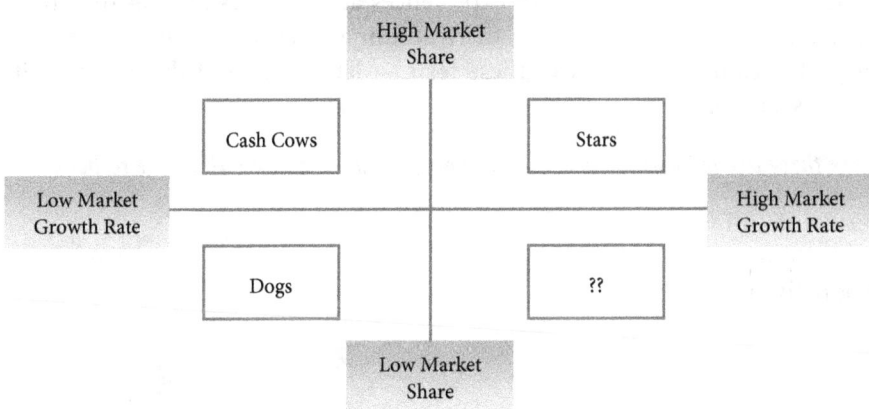

weak market share and a high growth rate, usually require cash investment so that they can become "stars."

The businesses in the high-growth quadrant with strong competitive position are those businesses that have opportunities for growth and profit. The "cash cows," with a strong competitive position and a low growth rate, are usually well established in the market, and such enterprises are in the position of making the products at low cost. Therefore, the products of such enterprises provide the cash needed for their operation. The "dogs" are businesses with a low growth rate and a weak market share position. These businesses are usually not profitable and generally should be disposed of.

The *Portfolio Matrix* was developed for large corporations with several divisions often organized around strategic business units (SBUs). While portfolio analysis was popular in the 1970s, it is not without its critics, who contend that it is too simplistic. Also, the growth rate criterion has been considered insufficient for the evaluation of an industry's attractiveness. Similarly, the market share as a yardstick for estimating the competitive position may be inadequate.

Setting the objectives

What should these objectives be then? There is only one answer: Objectives are needed in every area where performance and results directly and vitally affect the survival and prosperity of the business. These are the areas that are affected by every management decision. They decide what it means concretely to manage the business. They spell out what result the business must aim at and what is needed to work effectively towards these targets.

Objectives in these key areas should enable us to do five things: organize and explain the whole range of business phenomena in a small number of general statements; test these statements in actual experience; predict behavior; appraise the soundness of decisions when they are still being made; and enable practicing businesspeople to analyze their own experiences and, as a result, improve their performance. It is precisely because the traditional theorem of the maximization of profits cannot meet any of these tests — let alone all of them — that it has to be discarded.

There are three areas in which objectives of performance and results have to be set:

➤ Market standing
➤ Innovation
➤ Productivity

MARKET STANDING

Market standing has to be measured against the market potential, and against the performance of suppliers of competing products or services — whether competition is direct or indirect. "We don't care what share of the market we have, as long as our sales go up," is a fairly common comment. It sounds plausible enough, but it does not stand up under analysis. A company's sales may go up — and the company may actually be headed for rapid collapse. A company's sales may go down — and the reason may not be that its marketing is poor but that it is in a dying field and had better change fast.

Not only are absolute sales figures meaningless alone, since they must be projected against actual and potential market trends, but market standing itself has intrinsic importance. A business that supplies less than a certain share of the market becomes a marginal supplier. Its pricing becomes dependent on the decisions of the larger suppliers. In any business setback — even in a slight one — it stands in danger of being squeezed out altogether. Competition becomes intense. Distributors in cutting back inventories tend to cut out slow-moving merchandise. Customers tend to concentrate their purchases on the most popular products. And in a depression, the sales volume of the marginal supplier may become too low to give the needed service. The point below which a supplier becomes marginal varies from industry to industry. It is different in different price classes within the same industry. It has marked regional variations. But to be a marginal producer is always dangerous, and a minimum of market standing is always desirable.

To be able to set market standing objectives, a business must first find out what its market is — who the customer is, where he or she is, what he or she buys, what he or she considers value, what his or her unsatisfied wants are. On the basis of this study the enterprise must analyze its products or services according to "lines," that is, according to the wants of the customers they satisfy.

INNOVATION

For each line, the market must be determined — its actual size and its potential, its economics, and its innovating trends. This must be done on the basis of a definition of the market that is customer oriented and takes into account both direct and indirect competition. Only then can marketing objectives actually be set.

There are two kinds of innovation in every business: innovation in product or service, and innovation in the various skills and activities needed to supply them. Innovation may arise out of the needs of market and customer; necessity may be the mother of innovation. Or it may come out of the work on the advancement of skill and knowledge carried out in the schools and the laboratories by researchers, writers, thinkers, and practitioners.

PRODUCTIVITY AND "CONTRIBUTED VALUE"

A productivity measurement is the only yardstick that can actually gauge the competence of management and allow comparison between management of different units within the enterprise and different enterprises. Productivity includes all the efforts the enterprise contributes; it excludes everything it does not control.

Businesses have pretty much the same resources to work with. Except for the rare monopoly situation, the only thing that differentiates one business from another in any given field is the quality of its management on all levels. And the only way to measure this crucial factor is through a measurement of productivity that shows how well resources are utilized and how much they yield.

For developing a marketing plan, one needs to progress through the following steps.

THE MARKETING PLANNING PROCESS

Scanning the business environment and spotting the broad business opportunities

➤ Analyzing the environment and the technology options
➤ Analyzing the market and competition
➤ Customer sensing
➤ Analyzing all aspects relating to the product
➤ Pinpointing clearly the business opportunities that are available to the firm

Internal scanning of the firm

➤ Defining the mission of the firm; probing for what business are we in?
➤ Probing the strengths, distinctive capabilities, and limitations of the firm
➤ Deciding which of the spotted business opportunities should be pursued by the firm, after considering its aspirations, capabilities, strengths, and limitations
➤ Grouping the diverse business activities of the firm into a few distinct Strategic Business Units (SBUs)
➤ Evaluating the various businesses of the firm vis-à-vis the environment; using strategic planning models; locating the Stars, Cash Cows, Question Marks, and Dogs

Setting the marketing strategy

➤ Deciding which businesses have to be cultivated and nurtured, which ones merely need maintenance, which ones need phasing out
➤ Laying down the framework of marketing objectives in alignment with the corporate objectives
➤ Pinpointing the key areas in which marketing objectives have to be set; the key areas should include sales volume, profits, market share, service, and marketing innovation
➤ Assessing the current performance in the key areas
➤ Setting measurable and explicit goals in each key area

Developing the marketing strategy

➤ Selecting the target market
➤ Studying the customer, his profile, his characteristics, his buying motives, and his buying behavior
➤ Segmentation of the market using relevant bases
➤ Evaluating each of the segments
➤ Selecting the appropriate segments as the target market

Developing the marketing mix

➤ Deciding the approach with respect to each of the 4Ps
➤ Deciding the relative share/weight of each element in the total marketing effort
➤ Providing for the impact of the uncontrollable variables

Formulating the detailed functional plans and programs

➤ Sales forecast/sales plan
➤ Physical distribution plan
➤ Channel plan
➤ Advertising and sales promotion plan
➤ Sales force plan
➤ Sales organization plan

In order to create a realistic plan, the manager has to depend upon the marketing information system to gather the realistic data and plan on its basis. The same is made available through market research. In addition to the pre-plan information, through implementation of the plan, data has to be gathered and analyzed and continuously compared with the set plans, as shown in the diagram on the following page.

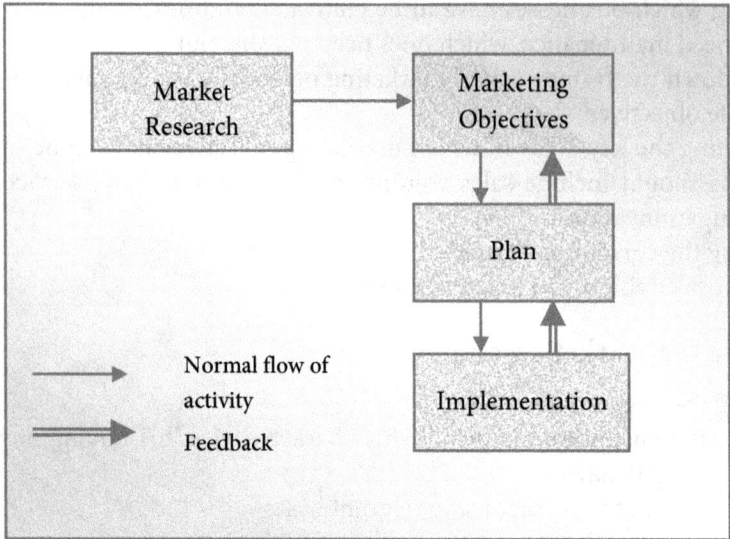

Market Research → Marketing Objectives

Marketing Objectives ↓↑ Plan

Plan ↓↑ Implementation

→ Normal flow of activity

⇒ Feedback

CHAPTER 4
Strategic Marketing Planning

After completing the strategic planning for its organization as a whole, management needs to lay plans for each major functional area, such as marketing or production. Of course, the organization-wide mission and objectives should guide planning for each function.

Strategic marketing planning is a five-step process:

1. Conduct a situation analysis.
2. Develop marketing objectives.
3. Determine positioning and differential advantage.
4. Select target markets and measure market demand.
5. Design a strategic marketing mix.

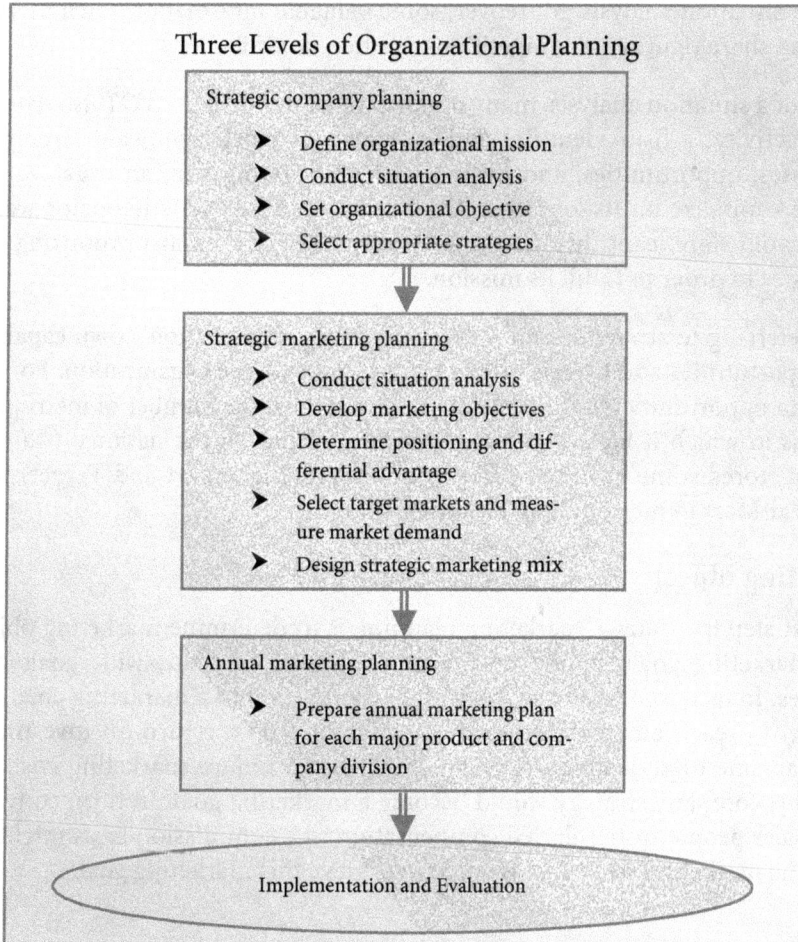

Three Levels of Organizational Planning

Strategic company planning

➤ Define organizational mission
➤ Conduct situation analysis
➤ Set organizational objective
➤ Select appropriate strategies

Strategic marketing planning

➤ Conduct situation analysis
➤ Develop marketing objectives
➤ Determine positioning and differential advantage
➤ Select target markets and measure market demand
➤ Design strategic marketing mix

Annual marketing planning

➤ Prepare annual marketing plan for each major product and company division

Implementation and Evaluation

Situation analysis

The first step in strategic marketing planning — *Situation Analysis* — involves analyzing where the company's marketing program has been, how it has been doing, and what it is likely to face in the years ahead. Doing this enables management to determine if it is necessary to revise the old plans or devise new ones to achieve the company's objectives.

Situation analysis normally covers external environmental forces and internal non-marketing resources (such as R&D capabilities, finances, and skills and experience levels of personnel) that surround the marketing program. A situation analysis also considers the groups of consumers served by the company, the strategies used to satisfy them, and key measures of marketing performance.

As the basis for planning decisions, situation analysis is critical. But it can be costly, time-consuming, and frustrating. For example, it is usually difficult to extract timely, accurate information from the "mountains" of data compiled during a situation analysis. Moreover, some valuable information, such as sales or market share figures for competitions, is often unavailable.

As part of a situation analysis, many organizations perform a *SWOT assessment*. In this activity, a firm identifies and evaluates its most significant strengths, weaknesses, opportunities, and threats. To fulfill its mission, an organization needs to capitalize on its key strengths, overcome or alleviate its major weaknesses, avoid significant threats, and take advantage of the most promising opportunities in order to fulfill its mission.

We're referring to strengths and weaknesses in an organization's own capabilities. Opportunities and threats often originate outside the organization. For example, an opportunity identified by Wal-Mart is the large number of metropolitan areas in which it has no stores. However, a threat to the national chain of discount stores is the group of competitors (including Kmart and Target) that await Wal-Mart in metropolitan locations.

Marketing objectives

The next step in strategic marketing planning is to determine marketing objectives. Marketing goals should be closely related to company-wide goals and strategies. In fact, a company strategy often translates into a marketing goal. For example, to reach an organizational objective of a 20% return on investment next year, one organizational strategy might be to reduce marketing costs by 15%. This company strategy would become a marketing goal. In turn, converting all sales people from salaried compensation to a commission basis might be one of the marketing strategies adopted to achieve this marketing goal.

We already know that strategic planning involves matching an organization's resources with its market opportunities. With this in mind, each objective should be assigned a priority based on its urgency and potential impact on the marketing area and, in turn, the organization. Then resources should be allocated in line with these priorities.

Positioning and differential advantage

The third step in strategic marketing planning actually involves two complementary decisions about how to position a product in the marketplace and how to distinguish it from competitors. Positioning refers to a product's image in relation to directly competitive products as well as other products marketed by the same company. For example, given rising health consciousness among many consumers, manufacturers of mayonnaise, corn oil, and other food products recognized the need to introduce products that would be perceived as more wholesome. CPC International is trying to position its Hellmann's Dijonnaise, which combines no-fat mustard with mayonnaise ingredients (but no egg yolks) as a healthful and tasty product.

After the product is positioned, a viable differential advantage has to be identified. Differential advantage refers to any feature of an organization or brand perceived by customers to be desirable and different from those of the competition. At the same time, a company has to avoid a different disadvantage for its product. Consider Apple Computers. For many years, the Macintosh's user-friendliness represented a strong advantage for the product. Eventually, however, the Macintosh's relatively high prices created a disadvantage in relation to comparable IBM and Compaq computers.

Target markets and market demand

Selecting target markets is the fourth step in marketing planning. A *market* consists of people or organizations with needs to satisfy, money to spend, and the willingness to spend it. For example, many people need transportation and are willing to pay for it. However, this large group is made up of a number of segments (that is, parts of markets) with various transportation needs. One segment may want low-cost efficient transportation, for instance, while another may prefer luxury and privacy. Ordinarily, it is impractical for a firm to satisfy segments with all different needs. Instead, a company targets its efforts on one or more of these segments. Thus a *target market* refers to a group of people or organizations at which a firm directs a marketing program.

In a new company, management should analyze markets in detail to identify potential target markets. In an existing firm, management should routinely examine any changes in the characteristics of its target markets and alternative markets. At that point, management should decide to what extent and in what manner to divide total markets and then pursue only those segments that show the best potential for successful marketing.

A firm may select a single segment as its target, as was done by the publisher of the highly specialized trade magazine, *Progressive Grocer*. In contrast, McGraw-Hill aims its periodical, *Business Week*, at several market segments. Target markets must be selected on the basis of opportunities. And to analyze its opportunities, a firm must forecast demand (that is, sales) in its target markets. The results of demand forecasting will indicate whether the firm's targets are worth pursuing or whether alternatives need to be identified. We'll take a look at demand forecasting later in this chapter.

Marketing mix

Next, management must design a *marketing mix*, which is the combination of product, how it is distributed and promoted, and its price. These four elements together must satisfy the needs of the organization's target markets and, at the same time, achieve its marketing objectives. Let's consider the four elements and some of the concepts and strategies.

PRODUCT

Strategies are needed for managing existing products over time, adding new ones, and dropping failed products. Strategic decisions must also be made regarding branding, packaging, and other product features, such as warranties.

PRICE

Necessary strategies pertain to locations of customers, price flexibility, related items within a product line, and terms of sale. Also, pricing strategies for entering a market, especially with a new product, must be designed.

DISTRIBUTION

Here, strategies involve the management of the channels by which ownership of products is transferred from producer to customer and, in many cases, the systems by which goods are moved from where they are produced to where they are purchased by the final customer. Strategies applicable to middlemen, such as wholesalers and retailers, must be designed.

PROMOTION

Strategies are needed to combine individual methods such as advertising, personal selling, and sales promotion into a coordinated campaign. In addition, promotional strategies must be adjusted as a product moves from the early stages to the later stages of its life. Strategic decisions must also be made regarding each individual method of promotion.

The four marketing mix elements are interrelated; decisions in one area often affect actions in another. To illustrate, design of a marketing mix is certainly affected by whether a firm chooses to compete on the basis of price or on one or more other elements. When a firm relies on price as its primary competitive tool, the other elements must be designed to support aggressive pricing. For example, the promotional campaign likely will be built around a theme of low prices. In non-price competition, however, product, distribution, and/or promotion strategies come to the forefront. For instance, the product must have features worthy of a higher price, and promotion must create a high quality image for the product.

Each marketing mix element contains countless variables. For instance, an organization may market one product or many, and they may be related or unrelated to each other. The products may be distributed through wholesalers, to retailers without the benefit of wholesalers, or even directly to final customers. Ultimately, from the multitude of variables, management must select a combination of elements that will satisfy target markets and achieve organizational and marketing goals.

Annual marketing planning

Besides strategic planning for several years into the future, more specific, shorter term planning is also vital. Thus, strategic marketing planning in an organization leads to the preparation of an annual marketing plan. An annual marketing plan is the master blueprint for a year's marketing activity for a specified organizational division or major product. Note that it is a written document.

A separate plan normally should be prepared for each major product and company division. Sometimes, depending on a company's circumstances, separate plans are developed for key brands and important target markets. As the name implies, an annual marketing plan usually covers one year. However, there are exceptions. For instance, because of the seasonal nature of some products or markets, it is advisable to prepare plans for shorter time periods. For fashionable clothing, plans are made for each season, lasting just several months.

PURPOSES AND RESPONSIBILITIES

An annual marketing plan serves several purposes:

➤ It summarizes the marketing strategies and tactics that will be used to achieve specified objectives in the upcoming year. Thus, it becomes the "how to do it" document that guides executives and other employees involved in marketing.

➤ The plan also points to what needs to be done with respect to the other steps in the management process, namely, implementation and evaluation of the marketing program.

➤ Moreover, the plan outlines who is responsible for which activities, when they are to be carried out, and how much time and money can be spent.

The executive responsible for the division or product covered by the plan typically prepares it. Of course, all or part of the task may be delegated to subordinates.

Preparation of an annual marketing plan may begin nine months or more before the start of the period covered by the plan. Early work includes necessary research and arranging other information sources. The bulk of the work occurs one to three months prior to the plan's starting date. The final steps are to have the plan reviewed and approved by upper management. Some revision may be necessary before final approval is granted. The final version of the plan or relevant parts of it should be shared with all employees who will be involved in implementing the agreed upon strategies and tactics. Since an annual plan contains confidential information, it should not be distributed too widely.

Recommended contents

The exact contents of an annual marketing plan should be determined by an organization's circumstances. For example, a firm in an intensely competitive industry would assess its competitors in a separate section. A firm in another industry would present this assessment as part of the situation analysis. Likewise, some organizations include alternative (or contingency) plans; others don't. An example of a contingency plan is the set of steps the firm will take if a competitor introduces a new product, as is rumored.

Annual marketing planning follows a sequence similar to strategic marketing planning. However, annual planning has a shorter time frame and is more specific both with respect to the issues addressed and to the plans laid. The major sections in an annual marketing plan are similar to the steps in strategic marketing planning.

In an annual marketing plan, more attention can be devoted to tactical details than is feasible in other levels of planning. As an example, strategic marketing planning might stress personal selling within the marketing mix. If so, the annual plan might recommend increased college recruiting as a source of additional sales people.

MARKET SEGMENTATION

The variation in customers' responses to a marketing mix can be traced to differences in buying habits, in ways in which the product or service is used, or in motives for buying. Customer oriented marketers take these differences into consideration, but they usually cannot afford to custom tailor a different marketing mix for every customer. Consequently, most marketers operate between the extremes of one marketing mix for all and a different one for each customer. To do so involves market segmentation, a process of dividing the total market for a product or service into several smaller groups, such that the members of each group are similar with respect to the factors that influence demand. A major element in a company's success is the ability to segment its market effectively.

Target market strategies

Let's assume that a company has segmented the total market for its product. Now management is in a position to select one or more segments as its target markets. The company can follow one of three strategies — market aggregation, single segment concentration, or multiple segment targeting. To evaluate the strategies, management must determine the market potential of each of the segments it has identified. But before a strategy is chosen, the potential of the identified segments must be determined. This calls for establishing some guidelines for target market selection.

Guidelines for selecting a target market

Four guidelines govern how to determine which segments should be the target markets. The first is that target markets should be compatible with the organization's goals and image. For years, many manufacturers resisted distributing their products through Kmart because of the chain's discount image. However, as Kmart achieved a high level of acceptability with consumers, image concerns seemed to disappear.

A second guideline consistent with our definition of strategic planning is to match the market opportunity represented in the target markets with the company's resources. In examining new product opportunities, 3M considered many options but chose the do-it-yourself or at-home improvement market due to the marketing economies that could be achieved. The firm's name was already well known to consumers, and the products could be sold through many of the retail outlets already selling 3M products. Thus, entering this market was much less expensive than entering a market in which 3M was inexperienced.

MARKET AGGREGATION		
Single Marketing Mix	→	One mass, undifferentiated market

SINGLE SEGMENT STRATEGY		
		Market Segment A
Single Marketing Mix	→	Market Segment B
		Market Segment C

MULTIPLE SEGMENT		
Marketing Mix A		Market Segment A
Marketing Mix B	→	Market Segment B
Marketing Mix C		Market Segment C

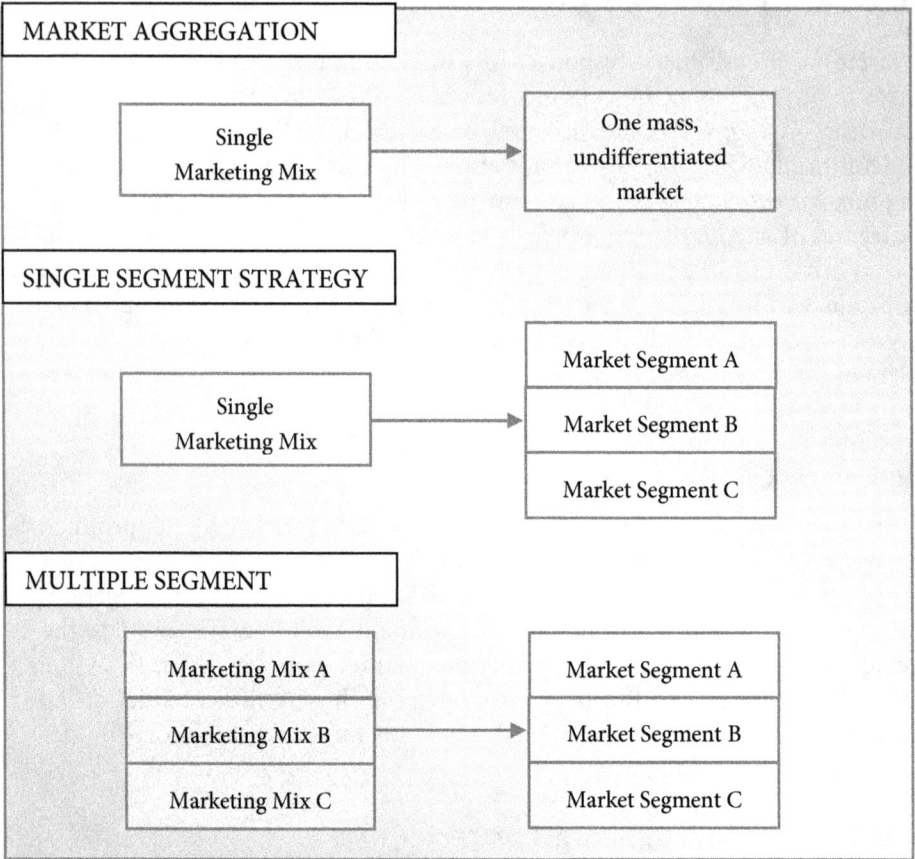

Over the long run, a business must generate a profit to survive. This rather obvious statement translates into our third market selection guideline. That is, an organization should seek markets that will generate sufficient sales volume at a low enough cost to result in a profit. Surprisingly, companies often have overlooked profit in their quest for high volume markets. Their mistake is going after sales volume, not profitable sales volume.

Fourth, a company ordinarily should seek a market where there are the least and smallest competitors. A seller should not enter a market that is already saturated with competition unless it has some overriding differential advantage that will enable it to take customers from existing firms. When Häagen Däz, a brand of premium ice cream, entered Europe and Asia in the late 1980s, it had little competition at the high end of the market. Because per capita ice cream consumption on these continents is well below that of the United States, many viewed the prospects of a high priced brand in a low usage market as not very attractive. However, Häagen Däz, with sales of over $500 million in 1991, proved the doubters wrong. It wasn't that consumers disliked ice cream; rather, many simply had not been exposed to a high quality version. By getting to the market first, Häagen Däz now has a significant advantage over later entrants.

These are only guidelines. A seller still has to decide how many segments to pursue as its target market, as we will see next.

Aggregation strategy

By adopting a *Market Aggregation Strategy*, also known as a mass market or an undifferentiated market strategy, a seller treats its total market as a single segment. An aggregate market's members are considered to be alike with respect to demand for the product. Therefore, management can develop a single marketing mix and reach most of the customers in the entire market. That is, the company develops a single product for this mass audience, it develops one pricing structure and one distribution system for its product, and it uses a single promotional program aimed at the entire market.

When is an organization likely to adopt the strategy of market aggregation? As we pointed out at the beginning of this chapter, it is not very common. Generally, it is selected after the firm has examined a market for segments and concluded that the majority of customers in the total market are likely to respond in very similar fashion to one marketing mix. This strategy would be appropriate for firms that are marketing an undifferentiated, staple product such as salt or sugar. In the eyes of many people, sugar is sugar, regardless of the brand, and all brands of table salt are pretty much alike.

The strength of a market aggregation strategy is in its cost minimization. It enables a company to produce, distribute, and promote its products very efficiently. Producing and marketing one product for the entire market means longer production runs at lower unit costs. Inventory costs are minimized when there is no (or very limited) variety of colors and sizes of products. Warehousing and transportation are most efficient when one product is going to one market. Promotion costs are minimized when the same message is transmitted to all customers.

The strategy of market aggregation typically is accompanied by the strategy of product differentiation in a company's marketing program. Product differentiation occurs when, in the eyes of customers, one firm distinguishes its product from competitive brands offered to the same aggregate market. Through differentiation, an organization creates the perception that its product is better than the competitors' brands, as when C&H Sugar advertises its product as "pure one sugar from Hawaii." In addition to creating a preference among consumers for the seller's brand, successful product differentiation can also reduce price competition.

A seller differentiates its product either (1) by changing some appearance feature of the product, such as the packaging or color, for example, or (2) by using a promotional appeal that features a differentiating claim. For example, various brands of aspirin each claim to be the most effective in relieving pain, although they all contain essentially the same ingredients.

Single segment strategy

A *Single Segment* (or concentration) *Strategy* involves selecting one segment from within the total market as the target market. One marketing mix is developed to reach this single segment. A company may want to concentrate on a single market segment rather than take on many competitors in the broader market. For example, Harley Davidson concentrates only on the super heavy weight motorcycle market. It does not produce small street bikes or offroad bikes. In contrast, Honda competes in all segments of the motorcycle market.

When manufacturers of foreign automobiles first entered the U.S. market, they typically targeted a single market segment. The Volkswagen Beetle was intended for the low price, small car market, and Mercedes Benz targeted the high income market. Today, of course, most of the established foreign car marketers have moved into a multi-segment strategy. Only a few, such as Rolls Royce and Ferrari, continue to concentrate on their original single segment.

A single segment strategy enables a seller to penetrate one market in depth and acquire a reputation as a specialist or an expert in this limited market. A company can initiate a single segment strategy with limited resources. And as long as the single segment remains a small market, large competitors are likely to leave it alone. However, if the small market should show signs of becoming a large market, then the big boys may jump in. This is exactly what happened in the market for herbal teas. Starting in 1971, Celestial Seasonings, then a small Colorado firm, specialized in this segment and practically owned the market for close to 10 years. But as herbal teas became more popular, this market segment began to attract major competitors, such as the Lipton Tea Company.

The risk and limitation of single segment strategy is that the seller has all its eggs in one basket. If the market potential of that single segment declines, the seller can suffer considerably. Also, a seller with a strong name and reputation in one segment may find it very difficult to expand into another segment. Sears, Roebuck, with an image as a retailer for the middle class was not successful when it tried to move into the market for expensive furs and designer clothing. Gerber was seen as a baby food company and was unable to market food in single serving quantities to adults.

Multiple segment strategy

Under a *Multiple Segment Strategy*, two or more different groups of potential customers are identified as target markets. A separate marketing mix is developed to reach each segment. For example, the maker of Bayer aspirin has decided that all consumers may not want to treat pain in the same way and so the firm produces the Bayer Select line of five non-aspirin, symptom-specific pain relievers. In segmenting the passenger automobile market, General Motors originally developed separate marketing programs built around its six major brands: Saturn, Chevrolet, Pontiac, Buick, Oldsmobile, and Cadillac. General Motors, in effect, tried to reach the total market for autos on a segmented basis. However, over the years the distinction between GM brands has diminished. Now there are Chevrolet models that overlap Buick and Pontiac models in price, appearance, and features. As a result, their target markets are no longer as distinctly defined, and the GM brands are competing with each other. To reduce the duplication, GM has decided to phase out the Oldsmobile brand name.

In a multiple segment strategy a seller frequently will develop a different version of the basic product for each segment. However, market segmentation can also be accomplished with no change in the product, but rather with separate distribution channels or promotional appeals, each tailored to a given market segment. Wrigley's, for example, targets smokers by promoting chewing gum as an alternative in situations where smoking is unwelcome. And Evian bottled water has broadened its market beyond athletes and fitness oriented consumers to other groups, including pregnant women and environmentalists.

A multiple, segment strategy normally results in a greater sales volume than a single segment strategy. It also is a useful strategy for a company facing seasonal demand. Due to lower summer enrollments, many universities market their empty dormitory space to tourists, another market segment. A firm with excess production capacity may well seek additional market segments to absorb this capacity.

Multiple segments can provide benefits to an organization, but the strategy has some drawbacks with respect to costs and market coverage. In the first place, marketing to multiple segments can be expensive in both the production and marketing of products. Even with today's advances in production technology, it obviously is less expensive to produce mass quantities of one model and one color than it is to produce a variety of models, colors, and sizes. And a multiple segment strategy increases marketing expenses in several ways. Total inventory costs go up because adequate inventories of each style, color, and the like must be maintained. Advertising costs go up because different ads may be required for each market segment. Distribution costs are likely to increase as efforts are made to make products available to various segments. Finally, general administrative expenses go up when management must plan and implement several different marketing programs.

CHAPTER 5
Consumer Behavior

The consumer is the most important factor in the entire buying process. It is the consumer whose actions determine the fate of the business and, therefore, it is very important that we understand how he or she behaves and why the consumer does what he or she does.

The essence of marketing is to create the customers. Profits will follow.

While going through the process of buying, a consumer responds to various cues, consciously and/or subconsciously. It is important to understand the reasons behind customer response to the cues.

The simplest model of consumer behavior is:

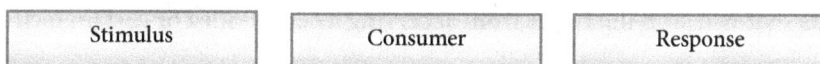

Stimulus	Consumer	Response

The consumer responds to various stimuli. Some of them are consciously offered to him by the marketers and some are offered by various factors that shall be discussed separately.

In response to these stimuli. the consumer will choose whether or not to buy the product. Therefore, it is important to understand what the various factors mean to the consumer.

THE Ps IN MARKETING

Product

The *product* itself, in terms of its utility as seen by the consumer, will stimulate him to buy.

Price

The *cost* of the product too will have its impact on the consumption of the product.

Place

The *place* where the product is available to the consumer. The nearer the location to the consumer, the higher the chances of them buying it, and the lesser chance that the consumer will try to find an alternative product to satisfy the need.

Promotion

How the *product is promoted* by the marketers will also have an impact on the way in which the consumer responds to the stimulus for the purchase. Sometimes it could be the utility of the product as advertised, it could be a gift being offered, it could be a discount being offered, or it could be an advertisement of the product, and so forth.

Paradigm

This is probably the single most important factor. *Paradigm* is the mindset, or a parental model, that directs the behavior of the buyer. It will often stall the buyer consuming the product. The buyer may have certain fixed ideas in his or her mind that are a result of the their past experiences as well as experiences of others around them. On the basis of these, the buyer will form his or her own set of arguments that will stop the buyer from accepting a certain idea or certain fact.

A case in point is detergent. Through the years, consumers in developing countries were conditioned to believe that if they wanted to remove oily stains on clothing, they would have to rub them vigorously with soap cakes and then scrub them vigorously with a brush. It was difficult for them to believe that simply immersing the clothes in soapy water and rubbing them gently would take care of the stains and clean the clothes. It took years before consumers began to use detergents on a widespread basis in many developing countries.

Similarly, it is believed that instant coffee lacks the freshness of taste and aroma of a filtered coffee. Hence, the advertiser uses an elderly model who will not drink anything but a filtered coffee, yet the elderly model is unable to differentiate between the filtered coffee and the instant coffee.

In both cases — the detergent and the instant coffee — the marketer is addressing the paradigm in the minds of the buyers that influences the decision to buy and consume the product.

WHY DO PEOPLE BUY?

People do not buy out of necessity alone. In buying, people articulate a vision of good life. This vision lacks clarity and, therefore, can be influenced.

A social scientist named Abraham Maslow defines the five types of basic needs of an individual. They are:

Maslow's Hierarchy of Needs

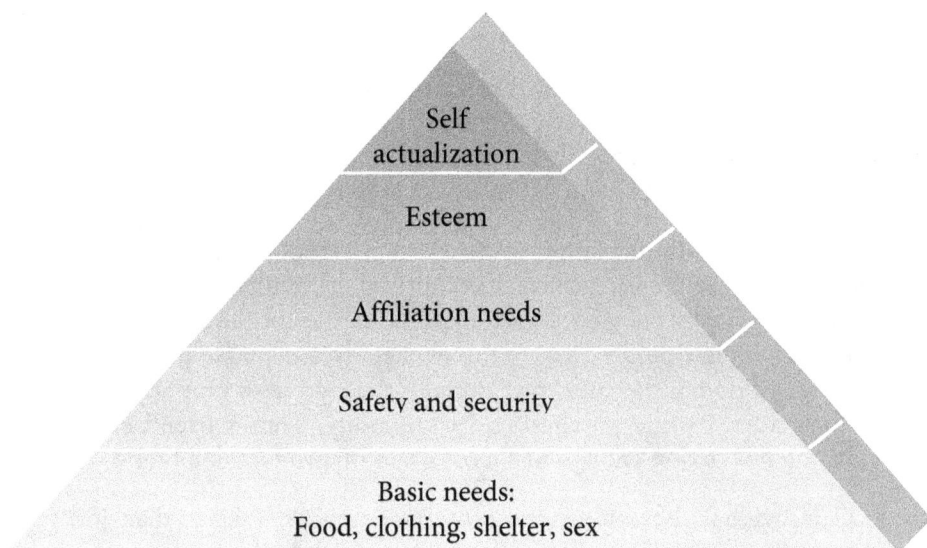

```
                    Self
                 actualization

                    Esteem

               Affiliation needs

              Safety and security

                  Basic needs:
           Food, clothing, shelter, sex
```

Maslow says that an individual goes about satisfying his or her needs by establishing a priority system. Only after satisfying these basic needs would the individual go about satisfying other needs. However, even in satisfying the basic needs there are various factors that are at play. For instance, let's examine the basic need for food. Hunger can be satisfied by intake of food in suitable form — it can be cooked at home, and here, too, we have many options to choose from — what dish to prepare, how to prepare it, what ingredients to use, etc. Alternatively, we can purchase cooked food from a restaurant and consume it to satisfy the need for food. But in a restaurant, there is also a wide range to choose from. We say that these places cater to different tastes of people as well as different paying abilities of people. A food item costing a few dollars in a certain restaurant may cost many more dollars in some other restaurant, yet both the restaurants flourish.

That is because in going to an expensive restaurant, we are also paying for the decor, the treatment that we receive from the employees of the restaurant, and possible luxuries offered such as piano music accompaniment or outdoor café dining — in short, the esteem we feel we have gained in the process itself.

Maslow further states that so long as we are deprived of the higher level needs, those of love, esteem, and self-actualization, we are motivated to satisfy them and will try to seek the satisfaction in some form or another.

FACTORS INFLUENCING THE DECISION TO BUY

Social factors

Human beings are social animals. Our behavior patterns, likes, and dislikes are influenced to a great extent by the people around us. More often than not, we do things that are socially acceptable; those who do things that are not accepted by the society around them are often viewed differently.

People frequently seek confirmation of those around them. These are called *reference groups*. The reference group is comprised of neighbors, friends, co-workers, etc. — typically people who are at the same level of the social ladder as the individual. People would rather do things that are acceptable to their reference group. In so doing, the consumer imitates their group a number of times or seeks their advice while purchasing a commodity. That a friend or a co-worker is using it is reason enough to choose a certain product or a brand.

Almost all individuals have a general sense of living lives lesser than justice might dictate. They often believe they belong at a much higher rung on the social ladder, but the limitations in their environments have kept them from being where they deservedly should be. This could mean a higher place in the organization or more respect from society. Therefore, the individual tries to imitate the buying behavior of people at the position he or she aspires to be. These are known as *aspirational groups*. People will often buy and use things that are used by their boss at the office or because the marketer tells them that a certain individual who enjoys a respectable position in society is using that product.

Family factors

An individual may want to imitate the behavior of his or her reference or aspirational group, but may only do so if his family would accept that behavior. Family influences hold a significant place in the buying behavior, alongside the social factors.

An individual typically lives through two families: family of orientation and family of procreation.

Family of orientation: The family in which a person is born is his or her *family of orientation*. The influence of his or her own parents that reflects in an individual's upbringing has a significant effect on that individual's buying habits. For instance, an individual coming from an orthodox vegetarian family may not consume meat or egg even though he or she may appreciate its nutritional value.

Family of procreation: Typically formed by the individual, the spouse of the individual, and the children of the union. After marriage, an individual's purchasing habits are likely to be influenced by the spouse, so the priorities change. Not only that, but as the marriage gets older, people settle into certain roles. For instance, decisions related to health of the children may be made by the mother; while decisions related to investments may be taken on by the husband.

Personal factors

In all of this, an individual always attempts to maintain their own identity. This reflects a person's choice of lifestyle — his or her likes and dislikes. The lifestyle of a person is a reflection of the culture he or she belongs to and the values held. An individual's age also plays a significant role. As the age advances, needs as well as priorities continue changing.

Other personal factors include an individual's occupation and economic condition.

PERSONALITY

Buying is usually related to the buyer's self-image. The buyer will purchase and consume the goods that satisfy the buyer's perception of his or her self-image.

Motivational Factors

Motive is a pressing need that a person is trying to satisfy. This pressure of need will create tensions that will lead to a search for ways to reduce those tensions. This search may lead an individual to a product.

These factors are then translated into wants. An individual will purchase to satisfy two wants: the primary or core wants and the secondary wants.

	Core Want	Secondary Want
Glasses	Protection to eyes	Does it look good?
Shoes	Protection to feet	Elegance

As explained by Maslow's hierarchy of needs, the customer will establish the customer's own priority system in satisfying these wants. This priority is affected by the satisfaction of basic needs, the constraints on income, and the availability of the product.

Presuming that the individual has satisfied basic needs and has the necessary economical resources to buy the product, the place plays a very important role.

It is the marketer's responsibility to make the product available at a location that the buyer can reach easily to make the purchase of the product.

To determine the effect of the product on satisfaction of the need and/or want of the product, the buyer has to possess, consume, and use the product.

However, simply wanting the product may not be sufficient reason to lead the buyer to purchase. Sometimes a buyer may want a product but may not buy it, for the reasons explained above, yet sometimes he or she may buy a product without really needing it.

A want for the product can remain latent when the benefits of the product are unknown to the user. It is the marketer's responsibility to increase the awareness in the minds of the buyer. Also, the want may remain passive when the buyer is aware of the benefits but has inhibitions towards buying. For instance, the buyer may be aware of the nutritional value of eating meat but may be a vegetarian by upbringing and, therefore, hold inhibitions towards the consumption of meat. Or the buyer may not buy because he or she lacks the necessary financial resources, or because of a commitment made (e.g., to stop smoking) or other commitments (e.g., timely repayment of some loan).

To arouse the latent wants by making the customer aware of the product benefits, or by converting the passive wants into sale, the firm needs an excellent manufacturing base that is capable of producing and delivering the product that addresses and satisfies such aroused wants — in short, the product that delivers the promises that are made.

The marketplace is full of "me too" products — the products that are similar to each other and address the same needs. At such times it becomes necessary to 'differentiate' the products from the competition. The products are so differentiated by offering a different benefit to the buyer. This benefit could be in terms of taste, choice of colors, price, etc.

Not always would a customer perceive the differentiated benefit as important. At such times, the customer will buy out of:

➤ Habit
➤ Picking
➤ Liking

The *habitual* consumers of a competing product can be converted by offering additional benefits vis-à-vis the product being used. To enhance the *pick*, the familiarity of the product needs to be increased. This can be done through advertising, organizing prominent displays, etc. Attractive packaging can make the product prominent as well as *likable*.

SIGNIFICANT CUES FROM PRODUCT

Quality

Quality is a subjective concept. What is good quality to one individual may not be the same to somebody else. More often than not, the term *quality* is equated to specification of the product and whether or not the product conforms to these specifications. Here, too, the requirements of certain features in the product may change from individual to individual, depending on the use for which the product is going to be put. Therefore, we have to take away the subjectivity from the definition of *quality*. In an effort to do so, Dr. J.M. Juran, the *Quality* expert has chosen to define the term *quality* as *fitness for use.* If the product satisfies the purpose for buying it and is fit to use for the said purpose, then the product is a *Quality Product.*

Price

Purchase of the product is influenced by attraction of the product and the price of it. The price of the product may outweigh the attraction, and then the customer may look for cheaper alternatives. The concept of price is relative. The price may inhibit buying not because the customer does not have the ability to pay but because the buyer may be unwilling to pay.

Depending upon the benefit that the customer seeks, the customer has a definite cost benefit equation in his or her mind. To the marketer, the maximum obtainable price will depend upon the customer's dependence on the product.

When the products are more or less similar, the customer will categorize them on price. It is the marketer's responsibility to minimize the impact of price on the customer. Therefore, it is said that:

➤ Cost is a *fact*
➤ Price is a *policy*

There is no such thing as *high price* or *low price*. The perception will vary from individual to individual, though often *high price* is equated to *high quality* and *low price* is equated to *low quality.*

Quality is the value that the customer attaches to the utility of a certain product that will be detrimental to the impact of the price.

In the case of fashion goods, for instance, *high price* would mean *exclusivity* and may have a positive effect. Moreover, when the performance of the product is critical, *high price* will still attract buyers.

Though reaction to *low price* is *low quality*, sales and bargain offers will still attract buyers. They suggest regret if the opportunity is lost.

Promotion

When the products are similar, *promotion* plays a significant role. Promotion tries to create a separate identity for the product in the minds of the customers.

Effective promotion can be achieved by making customers aware of the benefits that can be derived from the usage, the price, and the quality of the product. Promotion may also take the role of an adviser. For products that are purchased infrequently, such as consumer durables, it may subtly suggest imitation of others by giving references of individuals who have already purchased the product. Or the promotion may try to attract buyers through gifts and discounts. This is where adverting also plays a significant role. Advertising is basically designed to motivate the buyer in purchasing the product.

OTHER ASPECTS OF CONSUMER BEHAVIOR

Perception

An individual sees things as he or she wants to see them, by selecting and understanding the available information, and by creating a meaningful whole out of them. These perceptions are an outcome of values, beliefs, attitudes, and other experiences — his or her own or those of others around the buyer. These perceptions contribute to paradigms but may also have a positive effect on buying. For instance, a common perception is that anything that is Japanese is of excellent quality. That is why claims such as "Made in Japan" attract buyers.

Learning

It is a continuous process of changes in behavior that arise out of experiences that an individual has.

Beliefs and attitudes

Belief is a feeling about. something being real or true. It may arise from knowledge, opinion, or faith. Attitude is a way of thinking, feeling, or behaving.

Decision to buy

It is important to understand:

➤ What is purchased?
➤ What is the objective to purchase?
➤ Who is purchasing?

- How is the product purchased?
- On what occasion is it purchased?
- From where it is purchased?
- Buying is done to solve a problem.

STAGES IN BUYING

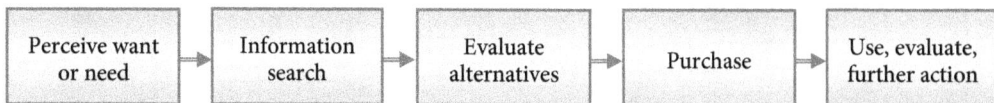

Perceive want or need	→	Information search	→	Evaluate alternatives	→	Purchase	→	Use, evaluate, further action

Stage 1: Perceive want or need

The perception of need triggers the buying process. These triggers could be internal, such as hunger, or external such as liking the design of a shirt or a pair of shoes The marketer must understand the source of such a trigger.

Stage 2: Information search

The buyer then starts gathering information as to how the buyer's triggered need or want can be satisfied.

Stage 3: Evaluate alternative

Having researched and discovered more than one way to satisfy the want or need, the buyer will evaluate them on the basis:

- Production attributes, such as quality, price, appeal, effectiveness, etc.
- Utility

Stage 4: Purchase

This evaluation leads the buyer into making a decision to buy. This decision is influenced by the attitudes of others as well as the buyer's own preferences.

Stage 5: Use, evaluation, and further action

The product is then consumed and evaluated compared with perceived satisfaction that led to the purchase in the first place. Satisfaction may lead to repeat purchases later on, whereas dissatisfaction may lead to no further purchase of the product, informing others of a negative experience, or taking action, such as complaints or legal actions.

In the case of new products (received by the market for the first time) or new brands (existing product in the market but introduced by a different company or the same company) it is essential to create awareness of the product, generate interest, and encourage purchase or trials.

In any market there is a certain set of customers who eagerly adopt a new product or a new brand. These buyers, if opinion leaders, pave the way for consumption of the product by others.

CHAPTER 6
Marketing Management and the Behavioral Environment

SOME ASPECTS OF CULTURE

A discussion of marketing and culture might appropriately begin with some indication of what it is we are trying to identify as cultural behavior. Culture is a "fuzzy" concept and hard to pin down.

The essence of the culture of a group is that the underlying values and the day-to-day behavior patterns developed to achieve such values are taken for granted, although some members of the group with a different perspective may deviate from the norm. How much deviation a society can tolerate is an open question. In times of change the cultural stress generated is a test of the strength of the old ways and the ability of the "in" group to assimilate or block the new. This strain to coherence is present regardless of the level of sophistication.

Obviously, not all societies develop the same adjustments to each other and to their environment. Some societies believe that supernatural forces alien to man cause floods, drought, pestilence, and disease. As it is the disposition of the gods that control such events, these people use feasts, sacrifices, and elaborate ritualistic ceremonies to appease their gods. Other societies consider such occurrences to be the result of natural forces and therefore develop sciences of agronomy, meteorology, and medicine to cope with their environment. In each, a socially accepted pattern of behavior is worked out. The ceremonies and symbols, the clothing and equipment, the prayers and the medicines, the fertilizers and the scarecrows in the fields, all are part of the patterned behavior employed by man in trying to deal with environmental forces, social and natural, that threaten him. Not all behavior imprints itself on succeeding generations. The patterns that do get "passed on" form the basis of culture.

Again, we find ourselves asking, *What is the nature of culture?* For some, culture has to do with believing, feeling, and thinking. *Are the people of a society materialistic or spiritualistic? Do they value tradition rather than innovation? Are they aggressive or passive? What aspirations are they striving toward?* The questions imply different values, different cultures. For others, culture is behavior, as evident in the widespread and persistent pattern of behavior observable in one country as contrasted with another. In going about their daily activities, people react in a predictable manner, thus making communal life possible. Culture in this sense is behavior that is taken for granted, which is expected.

For still others, it is the interplay of values and behavior that defines culture. The tendency to place undue, if not complete, emphasis on behavior — i.e., the customs and norms of a society — is categorized by Bidney as the "positivistic fallacy." On the other hand, to define culture in terms of norms and values and to ignore or minimize actual behavior is to commit the normative fallacy.

For those scholars who consider culture to include both behavior and norms, actions and ideals are interactive. Through child-rearing practices that include rewards and punishments, for example, adult personality traits are developed that produce similar day-to-day behavior in individuals, and the members of this society for the most part share similar goals and values which, in turn, give direction to their actions.

Observing the characteristic behavior patterns of a society and the shared beliefs of individuals, scholars have noted a central tendency. The "press" of custom tends to induce individuals to acquire and develop those beliefs, values, and abilities needed to perform successfully the life tasks that each generation inherits. It is not so much that John Doe eats three meals a day or drinks tea in the afternoon or has wine at each meal or dresses up on Sunday which is culturally significant, but that others see such actions as normal — not so much that there are churches, but that church-going is expected — not so much that there are butchers and bakers and candlestick makers, but that work is honorable.

SOCIAL CLASS

Modern, complex societies require that many goods and services be produced. To do this efficiently, they employ in varying degrees a division of labor so that the production of food, clothing, shelter, and other functions are performed by specialists. This division of labor is largely at the base of differential social behavior. We are, of course, not speaking here of one-man Robinson Crusoe or primitive societies, but of modern industrial nations, the essence of which is economic — specialization. In such societies, people are constantly evaluating themselves in relation to others; this appears to be a basic propensity. They see others as being the same or different from themselves, as having more or less desirable jobs, more or less money, education, possessions, or whatever. Man is a gregarious animal and expresses his needs in a social context.

The awareness that some groups of people have more in common, both psychologically and materially, than do others is the beginning of social class analysis. This awareness of groupings need not, by itself, lead to a ranking. However, in a truly classless society, either all would have to be doing the same thing or all things done would have to be evaluated equally. The first condition is no doubt approached in very small primitive societies where division of labor is minimal and land and tools are owned in common. Yet even here there is division — holy men vs. warriors, etc. The second condition appears simply to be contrary to fact. Through the division of labor, there is an assignment of jobs that leads to differing lifestyles, and not all jobs and lifestyles are perceived of as having equal value to either the individual or society. Thus, where there is division of labor, ranking occurs.

Marketing analysts have studied social groupings rather closely. The literature on social class familiar to marketing people is replete with such concepts as "upper-lower class," "working class," "elites," and "upward mobility." Lloyd Warner's studies have made a special contribution to the marketing vocabulary. His six-class model is widely used, although often with modifications. However, the fact that Warner used six classes in his Yankee City, in which others have found only two important classes, and that still others have adjusted their classes to accommodate "star" groups or "over– or underprivileged" groups, means that any market segmentation by social class has to be developed with sophistication and caution. Warner's model of six classes cannot be applied in a generalized fashion to all communities. In any event, the number of social classes in a given community is a question of ranking and cutting the data. Researchers have tackled this differently or not at all. The latter view society as a continuum with no clear grouping or with greater variations within than between grouping. This has raised speculation in many minds as to the "real nature" of social classes. Some ask whether there are classes at all. If so, do they really exist "out there" or are they merely constructs of the research that produced them, to be used as "models" by which to understand and organize the social order.

It is not our purpose here to enter into the ideological or methodological controversies that exist in the sociological literature on social class analysis. The degree of "reality" possessed by social classes is to be judged for marketing research purposes by how well such an analytical approach makes sense of the social behavior observed.

Limits to the concept

The hope of marketing managers is to use social class techniques to segment the market in clusters of people having similar wants, tastes, values, attitudes, lifestyles, purchasing power, and willingness to purchase — a tall order. In reality, of course, there is no one who is just like a person but the person himself. For a perfect match of offerings to individual tastes, every individual is a market segment, although a segment too small to be catered to except on a custom basis. Parisian high fashion houses traditionally come close to this. However, only a very small percentage of production is custom-made. The ever-present problem for most firms is a tradeoff between customization of production and developing market segments of an economically profitable size. For national producers of consumer perishables such segments are large indeed, encompassing a very sizable portion of the mass market, i.e., "bread and butter" items. For other types of products — mostly shopping and specialty goods — the economically profitable segment is still large but may vary considerably on either a national, regional, or metropolitan basis.

As we have seen, social classes, if they could be reasonably well identified and reached, would be one way of segmenting markets — markets that would have fairly homogeneous characteristics with greater interclass than intraclass differences. Unfortunately, the findings to date in social class analysis hardly appear sophisticated enough to delineate classes so specifically that marketing managers know what to produce, for whom, at what price, using what media, and so on.

However, despite caveats, social class analysis has something to offer and can supply fruitful guides to marketing action — some specific, some rather directly helpful, and some so general as to offer only background orientation to sharpen areas for further research.

SOCIAL CLASS AND MARKETING ANALSIS

There are several studies on differential attitudes by class toward product types and product quality. Burleigh Gardner, for example, states that those in the upper-middle class tend to spend a larger proportion of their income for housing, furnishings, and cultural amusements than the lower class, while the latter group spends a larger proportion for food, sports, and immediate pleasures.

Rainwater, Coleman and Handel state that the core values around which the life of the workingman's wife revolves are a search for physical and economic security, a need for respectability and affection, an effort to escape household labor, and the urge to "pretty up" her environment. "Out of such striving, and the inevitable compromises which must be made as they conflict, derive the everyday purchasing decisions which ring cash registers in the supermarket, the department store, the drug store." Translated into marketing policies this means, as applied to the lower classes, a market for appliances, sturdy home furnishings and equipment, gadgets, and knickknacks for adornment. To the extent that Coleman's "overprivileged" and Martineau's "star" groups are present at this level, the quality and types of products could be upgraded.

It is well known that messages are received selectively. People are not aware of the same stimuli, even in their common environment. Some environmental information is not noticed at all and some is background of which people are barely aware, while some stimuli are highlighted and taken account of in their behavior.

The interpretation an individual puts on what he or she selectively perceives is a function of past experience. For example, the differential perception due to different social class experiences was, of course, at the base of the Martineau store identification. In the eyes of upper-class individuals, very heavy type, bold displays of prices are in bad taste and denote a store that is "beneath" them. For working-class people, on the other hand, such stores are places for "good buys."

Marketing people need to be reminded that media messages, whether television, magazine, newspaper or whatever, may be received in quite garbled form and may, in fact, not pass into awareness at all. There is always the possibility that the symbolism of messages will be lost to some classes. As one author put it: "A perfume ad showing an anthropological mask and swirling colors is likely to be incomprehensible to many working class women, whereas metro city readers will at least pretend they grasp the symbolism."

Montrose Sommers' study explores a related phenomenon — the ability of a person to see through the eyes of another. Using a "self-perception technique," subjects were asked to describe not only themselves but also another person (as though they were that "other"). One of the several findings of this complex study was that members of the higher strata groups demonstrated greater agreement in describing an "other" than did members of the lower strata. This would imply that sales appeals to lower-class audiences based on emulation of high-strata individuals should be used with caution.

In general, these studies bring out a characteristic of social levels that is rather well known — that the ability to be facile with abstractions, to be objective, to be articulate, and to imagine oneself in the shoes of another increases with education, occupational status, and richness of home environment — all earmarks of social class level.

Too much can be made of specialized studies, but an overall direction is clear. Communication between classes is difficult. In the advertising world, as is well known if not always remembered, the "other," the audience, is the one to be kept in mind.

SOCIAL CLASS AND LEISURE

The use of leisure time according to social class has been reported by several authors. Clyde White, in his studies of social class differences in the uses of leisure in an Ohio county, indicates, for example, that the higher the social class, the less use of the home as a leisure center, the less church attendance, the less use of parks and playgrounds, the greater use of libraries, the less use of commercial amusements. And Alfred Clarke, in his Columbus, Ohio, study on leisure activities of males, reports the following (in part): The highest prestige groups attended plays, concerts, lectures, played bridge, studied, entertained at home. The lowest level watched television, fished, played cards other than bridge, drove their cars for pleasure, spent time in taverns and zoos, attended baseball games.

REFERENCE GROUPS AND "OTHERS"

Much of what we do can be seen to flow naturally from our surroundings. We act in ways that by and large make sense to friends, neighbors, work colleagues and, possibly, even our enemies. But not all of an individual's behavior is explainable by reference to the stimuli originating in the events and people that surround him.

The use of the term "reference group" arose largely to explain the behavior of individuals that appeared to deviate from what would be expected, given their immediate common environment. In any group there is a high probability that some of the actions of some individuals and even all of the actions of some individuals will "stand out." How does this deviate from the norms that appear to characterize the group at large? Who is trying to impress whom? If, as Thoreau once pointed out, a person out of step may be listening to "a different drummer," who is the other drummer?

Although the discussion that follows may seem to overemphasize the absent drummer, it should not be forgotten that most of our actions are taken in concert with our own primary, face-to-face groups. For the most part, we do listen to a common drummer. Social behavior is conditioned in childhood by the family and its influence is deep and long-lasting. Peer groups — those we see, talk to, and do things with every day — mold behavior as much as, if not more than, the family. However, if these were the only sources of social influence, it is doubtful whether the concept of reference groups would ever have developed. It is because people take cues for their behavior from, and emulate groups and individuals who are not in their immediate environment, that reference group analysis has developed in the manner it has.

Before proceeding further in this discussion of reference groups, it might be well to define briefly what is meant by the term and how it is used in the analysis of social behavior. In fact, as we shall point out, the word "group" in the term is in many ways unfortunate. Groups, as we shall see below, may not always be the reference point in reference group analysis. A fuller and more accurate understanding of the term will become evident as the discussion proceeds.

Reference relationships

There are three kinds of reference groups:

➤ groups which afford comparison points in making self-appraisals or judgments
➤ groups whose frame of reference is adopted for conduct, and
➤ groups to which one aspires

These may be groups in which an individual has membership and face-to-face interaction, or they may be at a distance and known only via television and other mass media, word of mouth, public reputation, and so on. In short, membership in a group is not essential to its use as a reference group, nor need one even aspire to membership. However, groups to which one does aspire may be strong reference groups indeed. Also, there are loose categories or collectives, possessing almost none of the characteristics of a group and whose members may even be unknown, which can serve as a reference "group" and define a situation so that present behavior is influenced. "Avant-garde," "fashion leader," "old-fashioned liberal" are categories or constructs that come to mind in this context. Some people are even influenced by an intangible, such as "posterity."

As mentioned above, the notion of reference covers more than groups. Hence, the "others" used as guides for action or as reference points may be an individual, such as a parent, a national leader, a trusted relative, a sports hero, or some "opinion leader." The point here is that a person can make comparisons, internalize values and norms, and organize his environment using a wide variety of "others." With this in mind, let us review briefly the character of groups discussed in the literature on reference group analysis and then turn to a short presentation of the non-group reference points, such as collectives, categories, reference individuals, and the like.

Group characteristics

If we are interested in the social environment that molds behavior, we must consider whatever it is that individuals "take into account" when they contemplate an act. Formal or organized groups quite obviously are "taken into account." Such groups are typically characterized by an awareness on the part of members that they are members; there are criteria for determining membership, and non-members know they are non-members. Some sort of structure with positions of leadership and followership are apparent, and there are various techniques or reward and punishment to motivate the members toward the group goals.

Formal groups are numerous. Religious, service clubs, labor organizations, and so on are, as a rule, formally structured. Even the family is a formal group in the eyes of the law. Such formal organizations constitute central reference points for the values, actions, and social behavior of many people. For some, however, even though formally members of such groups, their behavior is little influenced by their membership. Not only do individuals vary in their loyalty to and participation in such groups, but groups themselves often have conflicting values and behavior patterns. Even a single formal group, such as one's religion, may embody conflicting values.

Thus, not only may the norms of the church be at odds with the norms of the fraternity or work group, but the church itself may have acceptable values in one sphere — spiritual matters — but not in another sphere — divorce or family planning. It is quite understandable that when formal organizations take positions on several aspects of everyday living — morals, dress, recreation, character of associates, voting, and so on, members may well differ in their points of allegiance. If all formal groups had clear-cut norms and if all members were equally aware of these norms and abided by them, reference group analysis, while not rendered irrelevant, would be considerably simplified.

Thus, we can see that membership in a group per se does not tell us all that we would like to know about the use of that group as a reference point. Besides the formal groups discussed above, there are many informal groups that individuals consciously or unconsciously turn to for guidance in daily behavior. In work, play, and prayer, people draw upon some sources more than others for guidance and they may often reject the guidance of a formal group in favor of the norms of some loose coalition of friends or social leaders. Such "free" groups are hard to define. They may be of a rather permanent nature or they may come into being, group and regroup or fade away. It is often difficult to know who the members are of "cafe society," the "street corner gang," the "inner circle" of a church, corporation or political party, or the "elite" of a local society.

Of course, informal groups or loose coalitions, like formal groups, have varying degrees of influence over an individual's dress, occupation, residence, behavior patterns, and values. But whether an individual is "in" or aspires to be "in," they may constitute powerful reference groups.

Negative references

We have noted above the positive influences exerted by reference groups. There are also negative influences. An individual may be known not only by the company he or she keeps, so to speak, but by the company he or she rejects. Negative reaction to the speech, dress, habits, beliefs, and possessions of some groups or individuals can be a very strong influence on one's behavior. Not owning a television set, not going to certain events, not wearing specific apparel, and type of dress are positive acts in themselves and give evidence of what one is not. And such rejections, of course, indirectly define what one is.

Non-group references

The above discussion has centered on groups, either formal or informal, aspired to or rejected, and involving membership or non-membership. It has said little or nothing concerning non-group reference relationships alluded to earlier. In a study of reference phenomena, some note should be taken of the influence of "others" who do not fit into the classification of a group.

All people have behavior patterns they follow with more or less fidelity that are not oriented to groups but to loosely defined categories. Age bracket, educational level, sex, and income range are examples. Identification with such categories often helps define a situation or determine a decision to act. Thus, certain behavior occurs because one must "act one's age" or because it is "unbecoming to one's sex." Although the specific behavior involved may be acted out with awareness of some reference group proper, there is also behavior that is not consciously determined by such reference group pressure but is merely appropriate to a category one possesses as a condition of one's present existence.

Generalized others and significant others

Not usually part of reference group theory per se, but clearly within the broader application of Shibutani's reference relationships is the concept of the "generalized other." The "other" in this term does not refer to a specific person or group of people. Rather it refers to an idealized or imaginary "other" who epitomizes the generally accepted behavior of the community or group. When it is said that "people don't do that" or "they" won't approve of that, the reference to the "they" or the "people" is an appeal to a "generalized other." It is, in a sense, captured in the term "Keeping up with the Joneses" when the Joneses are not any particular Jones family. When communities and social groups become large and face-to-face, interaction is lost, there is a strong tendency to construct behavior patterns that "the other guy" is, in general, expected to follow. Social behavior in many situations is adjusted with such a "generalized other" reference point.

In contrast to the conceptualized "other" discussed above is what has been termed a "significant other." Such a person is a specific "other" and one whose behavior is accepted and internalized. Such a person may be a parent, a trusted relative, a colleague, an esteemed public figure — a person, in short, whose values and habits are deeply felt and made some part of the self. "Significant others" are those who really matter in shaping one's basic personality and behavior patterns.

Shibutani then went on to relate the reference individual to the interpersonal influence relationships that have been uncovered in the research on communication networks and the diffusion process — the diffusion of products, the diffusion of ideas, the diffusion of behavior patterns. Especially relevant are the concepts of the "opinion leader" and the "influential" as conceptualized in the work in the agricultural field, the drug industry, women's fashions, voting behavior, and so on. Reference individuals are those individuals whose opinions, advice, and behavior are used as comparison points and guidelines for personal behavior in the areas involved.

Reference groups, others, and marketing management

Reference group concepts, as such, have not been as important in marketing research as the concept of social class or some of the psychological concepts such as motivation or attitude, which will be taken up in later sections. While there have been a few studies centered directly on reference group analysis, such as the work reported below by Bourne, in most of the relevant marketing literature it has been secondary to other matters of more immediate interest to the authors. This is so probably for two reasons. First, but of less importance, is the simple fact that other areas of research, such as attitude or motivation, appear to many to have more relevance to marketing problems. Second, and probably of greater importance, is the present lack of any successful approach to the problem. We do not yet have the information that will really help in determining which kinds of groups are likely to be referred to by which kinds of individuals under which kind of circumstances in the process of making which decisions and of measuring the extent of this reference group influence.

Moreover, a trap to be avoided is circularity of reasoning, i.e., determining the relevant group from the behavior. In short, there is the problem of locating the "drummer." Despite these problems, something has been said on the subject of reference groups as an influence in decision making in marketing situations. And there is a considerable amount of literature on personal influence which, as we have seen, comes under the rubric of "reference individual." In general, researchers in the reference, field make little or no mention of whether the reference entities they are concerned with are groups, categories, individuals, or all of these.

Influence group, products, and brand

One of the statements concerning the influence of others is that in situations where objective criteria are absent, decisions of an individual are more likely to follow group norms — the "collective" opinion of these "others" — than to be made on independent, completely self-determined grounds. Venkatesan, in a controlled experiment involving a decision concerning men's suits, found evidence supporting this position. When pre-instructed confederates in a group openly selected suit B (from three identical suits labeled A, B, and C), the decisions of the individuals who were the subjects of the experiment followed that of the majority.

Venkatesan was also interested in a second hypothesis concerning group influence. In consumer decision-making situations where no objective standards are present, individuals who are exposed to a group norm and are induced to comply will show less tendency to conform to the group judgment.

In this experimental situation, the pre-instructed confederates of the researcher announced their choice of suit B by indicating that as "good guys" they would follow, "go along" with, the choice made by the first individual (a confederate). In this situation, however, there was some implication that the others (the uninstructed) should do likewise. In short, there was a slight effort toward coercion. In this new situation, the uninstructed individuals "tended either to be indifferent or to deliberately make a choice that would negate the effect of the group." Too much can be made of laboratory experiments, but Venkatesan's experiments are in the direction of a commonly observed marketing phenomenon — large numbers of consumers "follow the fashions" and emulate the choice of the majority, but with enough variation to display some individuality — a different color fabric or a special variation on the main theme.

Reference group, products, and brand

The best known of the works relating reference group influence to consumer behavior is that of Francis Bourne referred to previously. For Bourne, the requirement that must be fulfilled in order for a product to come under reference group influence is that it be conspicuous. And it must be conspicuous in two ways: it must be visible, and it must be identifiable by others; it must "stand out." For example, a man's necktie clearly fulfills the first requirement — it is visible, it is seen. However, in as much as "everyone" wears a necktie, there is nothing novel about it; it may or may not fulfill the second requirement of standing out. This depends on the kind of necktie, given the circumstances under which it is worn. An inconspicuous, business-type necktie, similar to those of one's colleagues, is one thing; a bright red tie at a funeral is quite another. People do not typically wear bright red ties to funerals. What would the "others" think? Hence, there is a relationship of conspicuousness to group reference influences.

Given the above conditions, Bourne's analysis is concerned chiefly with the question of the influence of others in the purchase of a product or in the choice of a particular brand or type of product, or both. Bourne suggests four possibilities (with examples) and charts them.

Products and brands of consumer goods may be classified by the extent to which reference groups influence their purchase.

Weak (−)	Reference group influence relatively	Strong (+)
➤ Clothing ➤ Furniture ➤ Magazines ➤ Refrigerator ➤ Toilet soap		➤ Cars ➤ Cigarettes ➤ Beer ➤ Drugs
➤ Soap ➤ Canned peaches ➤ Laundry soaps ➤ Refrigerator ➤ Radios		➤ Air conditioners ➤ Instant coffee ➤ TV
	Product	

Interpretation

PRODUCT PLUS (INFLUENCE OF OTHER IS STRONG)
BRAND OR TYPE PLUS (INFLUENCE OF OTHERS IS STRONG)

Examples mentioned are automobiles, cigarettes, certain prescribed drugs, and beer. Not all purchases of such products fall equally, or at all times, under the influence of reference groups. However, whether or not one smokes and the brand selected are often influenced by those with whom one smokes. In the case of beer, Bourne reports that others influenced both whether the product was used and whether premium or regular was chosen. (Brand choice was apparently not influenced, only type.)

PRODUCT PLUS (INFLUENCE OF OTHERS STRONG)
BRAND MINUS (INFLUENCE OF OTHERS WEAK)

Among other products mentioned here are air conditioners, television sets, and instant coffee. Whether such is the case now is an empirical question. As Bourne points out, when markets become saturated with a product, such products are no longer conspicuous in a relevant sense and tend to drop to the brand minus/product minus category described below.

PRODUCT MINUS (INFLUENCE OF OTHERS WEAK)
BRAND OR TYPE PLUS (INFLUENCE OF OTHERS STRONG)

In this category fall the products widely used — "everyone has one,"— such as clothing. One has no choice as far as the product is concerned so reference groups are not involved. However, types of clothing and brands are influenced by "others." Even the person who says, "I want to be different from all those other guys," is reference group oriented.

PRODUCT MINUS (INFLUENCE OF OTHERS WEAK)
BRAND MINUS (INFLUENCE OF OTHERS WEAK)

Products which have low social significance fall into this category. Illustrations given by Bourne are salt, laundry soap, and radios.

It should be pointed out that products are not static. The may well move into and out of the above classifications. For example, strong advertising programs can make a brand socially conspicuous and the saturation of markets as time goes on can diminish or even eliminate any tendency to think of "others" when making a purchase.

ASPIRATION REFERENCE GROUP
AND STATUS CONFLICT

An interesting study having to do with the status of druggists by Thelma McCormack affords some insight into one of the theoretical categories of reference group theory — the group aspired to. In this study of first-year students in a school of pharmacy, McCormack explored the ambivalent status as perceived by members of this profession. The pharmacist's dilemma lies in the fact that he receives a professional type of education, and so one of his status reference groups is the college-trained professional pharmacist. However, a large number of pharmacists anticipate owning outright or being the co-owner of a drugstore. This tends to lead pharmacists to look to the business world also as a status reference point. How do pharmacists stand as business leaders? But whatever the status of the pharmacist as a businessperson, it is being undercut by the changing nature of the retail structure as chain and department stores add drug departments.

It is within this environment that pharmacists wonder about their status. When asked to compare their status to other occupations, pharmacists tend to ally themselves with medical-scientific groups. However, from her data, McCormack inferred that there was a "tendency of pharmacists to vest more prestige in pharmacy than others would be willing to do." This would seem to indicate that the medical-scientist group was an aspiration reference group for pharmacists. It would appear that there are also social class connotations here. Scientists, physicians, surgeons, and the like probably move in higher social circles than do pharmacists and drugstore owners.

Earlier in the discussion of reference group analysis, Hyman was quoted as saying that the concept of reference group has been given considerable attention, but that no such attention had been given to the concept of reference individual. He suggested that the "influential" uncovered in the research on the flow of communication was a reference individual — a person to whom others looked for information, advice, or clues for behavior. A few observations are appropriate here about the link between the work on personal influence and the reference individual of Hyman's theory.

Before the research on personal influence, it was thought that communication via the mass media — radio, television, newspapers, and so on — reached audiences as masses. Masses were conceived as a collection of individuals in an atomistic, isolated relationship. That is, interpersonal communication between mass audience members was thought to be nil or, at the very least, so slight as to be ignored. From this point of view, mass media messages in newspapers and television broadcasts went directly from the communicator to the recipient individual, unmediated.

However, it became apparent as research progressed that interpersonal communication was present and in a rather schematic form. Information went through a network whose pattern made it clear that there were some individuals who had more to do with the process than others. In short, these were reference individuals — individuals who were "influential" and had personal influence in the network of communication.

Katz and Lazarsfeld, for example, uncovered this phenomenon in voting behavior and in decisions regarding fashion, food, and movie-going. The direction, in general, was from communicator to influential to the individual.

This is not to imply that people simply adopt directly the counsel of the "influential." Rather, it means that conversation, face-to-face, takes place within an interpersonal network, quite often within such primary groups as the family, neighbors, and work colleagues, but also without outsiders. In this two-step manner, opinions are formed, attitudes developed, and behavior influenced. Also, there was a selective process concerning sources of information. The mass media (impersonal) tended to inform while the influential (personal) tended to influence.

Personal influence, as would be expected, varied situationally depending on the area being studied. In the Katz and Lazarsfeld study of clothing, for example, young, unmarried girls were the influential. In adoption of a new drug, the influential were highly respected doctors, well integrated into the profession and better acquainted with "outside" affairs.

Research into the two-step flow in the communication process, especially in the area of the diffusion of innovations, has developed a much more elaborate network than outlined here. There are "locals" and "cosmopolitans," "early adopters" and "innovators," with varying degrees of influence in the sense of having followers and so on.

Recent work indicates that the two-step flow may need revision to allow for a multi-step process to take account of the possibility of individuals participating in different ways with their influential — a simple dyadic relationship may be too constrictive. However, our concern is not with the details and refinements of the flow of information, and personal influence studies in many areas of activity may contribute to reference analysis as it affects marketing behavior. And while more adequate research methods are required, present studies are contributing to a better understanding of the process.

The family

The study of the family in sociology encompasses many aspects of kinship and marriage relationships that receive little or no attention from marketing people. Sociologists working in this area examine such matters as the functional role of the family in relation to other societal institutions (religious, economic, political), the problem of marriage and divorce, the organizational structure of the family (extended or nuclear), the rites of passage in family life (weddings, christenings, the emergence of children from puberty to adult status), the family as an institution. Marketing people interested in the family have been concerned primarily with such topics as the family life cycle, family mobility, decision-making within the family, and rates of new family formation. Despite the differences of interest, there is appreciable overlap.

We will see to what extent marketing has made use of the concept of the family in analyzing market behavior. In considering market purchases it is often helpful to determine whether a purchase is related to family or to individual considerations. This is not meant to imply that goods are either one or the other; a single person may purchase a washing machine as well as a newly married couple. However, the demand for many classes of goods is closely related to family or individual purchasing. For example, the demand for home appliances, such as stoves, refrigerators, washing machines, etc., is geared to family use and to the formation of new families. The demand for motorcycles, tennis shoes, etc., may be more closely related to the number of individuals in a given age bracket and gender.

Furthermore, something obviously needs to be known about how families decide what, where, and when to buy. And this process can often be a complex affair. For example, it is important to know who in a family initiates the suggestion to purchase a product or service, who influences the decision one way or another, who actually makes the decision, who makes the purchase, and finally, who uses the product or service. Often, all of these steps in the process are carried out by one person. For example, one individual may initiate, decide, buy, and use a pack of cigarettes. On the other hand, in the purchase of a small child's toy, the grandmother may initiate the idea, the brothers and sisters may influence the decision, the mother may actually decide, and the father may finally purchase the item. In this situation, to whom does the seller direct his advertising message? Grandmother, children, mother, or father? In what media does the seller advertise and in what outlets does the seller distribute toys? Are toys, to the father, a convenience, shopping, or specialty good? Of course, the flow of influence and action would be quite different in the case of an automobile, a refrigerator, a breakfast cereal, or a computer.

CHAPTER 7
Motivation

Early texts in marketing, when dealing with motivation, reflected the then-current psychological writings on the subject. Typically, this took the form of a list of "instincts," "traits," or "drives," which were based either on bodily needs — food, water, sex, etc. — or on "emotions" such as fear and anger. Some of the earlier viewpoints are still held to be sound, and others have been replaced by research findings that view motivation in a more complex fashion. And, it must be added, the field is by no means a settled one. There are several approaches to the subject, and much research still needs to be done. About the only thing all parties are agreed on is the importance of the subject.

Speaking broadly, and somewhat imprecisely, there are two main approaches to motivation theory today. According to the first, motivation is grounded in the basic visceral ends; according to the second, which leans more toward social forces and environmental interaction, motivation is grounded in a rather wide array of interpersonal situations. While some of these approaches can be traced to body deficiencies, others appear far removed from the chemistry of the organism. At the base of this divergence in emphasis is the question of the number and character of innate or unlearned drives, and whether such basic drives can support the superstructure of motivated behavior required to cope with the social drives of modern life. Can we, for example, understand the drive for money in the same way that we understand the drive for food? Is the need for achievement or affiliation on the same footing as the need for water or food?

In as much as no theory of motivation denies the hunger or thirst or sex need and their homeostatic or self-regulating activities, a short resume of this part of the motivation process may better set the stage for an understanding of schemes that either builds on the basic drives or skirts them in developing alternative explanations.

Basic drives

The theories of motivation as a response to the basic visceral drives appear to rest essentially on the periodic nature of the organism's deficiency and the urge to restore equilibrium when that state is disturbed. Thus, the body must maintain a given set of conditions as to the sugar content of the blood, temperature of the body, water content of the system, and so on. If we assume a state where all necessary conditions are met, then the mere passage of time, and hence the using up of some of the necessary elements, will develop tissue tension or system deficiencies which are communicated to the organism; this results in activity calculated to secure what is necessary to replenish the deficiencies and restore the system to its original state. The drive for food or water is directed to a goal object and becomes the hunger motive or thirst motive. The process is homeostatic — it seeks to restore a previous state of equilibrium.

Further, these basic physiological or visceral drives are innate and unlearned. As we shall see later, many of those who derive the "higher level" motives, such as the need for prestige or the motivating effects of money reward, do so by positioning learned or conditioned drives based on these basic needs. Thus, an organism can be conditioned to respond to previously neutral stimuli such as a sound or a light when under the need-drive of one of the physiological tensions.

Extreme reliance on visceral tensions, or tissue deficiency theory, and the construction of a superstructure of learned drives by conditioning has led to varying degrees of dissatisfaction. Some have felt that it has required too complex an apparatus of learned drives for the basic drives to support. Others have felt that the chain of events from basic tissue end to highest level social motivation was too difficult to reconciling the theory with recent experiments indicating that an organism does not, in fact, need reduction or a quiet state of homeostatic equilibrium. Instead, a human being is thought to be a wanting animal all the time. He or she seeks novelty, excitement, or at least mild stimulation. Further, there is reason to believe that the need for affection, achievement, and so on, are themselves part of our original equipment. In any event, in examining this premise, we now turn to see what can be said about the newer developments in motivation theory. We will then take up the relationship between motivation theory and marketing problems.

Social and environmental drives

The transition from preoccupation in motivation theory with basic visceral drives to socially "higher-order" drives came about for several reasons. Chief among them perhaps was the fact that the homeostatic nature of the older theories, which said, in effect, that man seeks to reduce his drives, did not seem to square with the observation that a human being is, as we have noted previously, a very active animal indeed. It ignored the fact that action and interest do not languish when the individual is free from the pressure of cold, hunger, and fatigue. If we are to trust our observation, we have to conclude that among the primary needs is that of participating in the surroundings, and that it is as powerful as any we observe. The narrow confines of the basic drive approach caused some scholars to look further afield for the sources of needs or drives that become channeled into motives. It was not so much a denial of the salience of the body needs as a re-evaluation of their place in the tremendous range of human activities and a recognition of their inability to account adequately for much of social behavior. For example, we are not so much interested in a person's hunger for food in general as in his or her specific appetites, in the fact that the dehydrated body craves liquid, as in the particular craving of the individual for wine or coffee or tea.

The drives which arise from humanity's cultural and social environment are now the center of much motivational study. White, for example, states: "We need a different kind of motivational idea to account fully for the fact that man and the higher mammals develop a competence in dealing with the environment which they certainly do not have at birth and certainly do not arrive at simply through maturation." White's interest is in the fact that something seems to motivate humans even when all bodily needs are fully satisfied. Handling the everyday environment is, from this point of view, a primary motivation that the purely visceral drives alone cannot account for. There is an intrinsic need — the need to manipulate, to achieve some sort of dominance or mastery over, the tasks of dealing with the social milieu.

This, White postulates, is a need for "competence," a persistent drive to learn how to cope with circumstances satisfactorily. In short, even when no organic deprivation is present, feedback from attempts to deal with the adjustment problems of a situation reinforces behavior. Other researchers also have addressed themselves to this kind of need and behavior. There appears, in their view, to be an optimum level of "excitement" necessary, not too much and not too little. Monotony, the perfect equilibrium of the homeostatic state, is unpleasant. There is an attraction to activity that results in efforts to vary behavior and seek excitement of a mild nature. "Even when its primary needs are satisfied and its homeostatic chores are done, an organism is alive, active, and up to something." The successful businessperson who does not retire or the entrepreneur who seeks new risks finds these activities rewarding. The implication is that "all tissues can become seats of tension and thus participants in drive." Effective motivation is persistent and ever present in a problem-solving, necessarily active environment.

Thus, while giving a place to the need-deprivation drives that hinges on thirst and hunger, this view widens the base of motivation to include the encompassing need to be competent in interacting with the environment.

Need for achievement

The studies of McClelland have recognized a motivational element in the need for achievement. The need for achievement varies among individuals and is characterized by the desire to have personal responsibility and credit for action, to set moderate goals with calculated risks, and to want concrete feedback of performance. Individuals who spend a lot of time thinking about problems and how to solve them, inventing better ways to do things, and so on, exhibit this achievement motive. The need to achieve is not, as far as business is concerned, related directly to profits or monetary reward. The achiever is basically motivated to accomplishing things personally. This type of person is found not only in the business world but also in government or wherever one can have responsibility and reaction to his or her performance."Apparently, a manager working for the Bureau of Ships in the Department of the Navy spends as much time thinking about achievement as his or her counterpart in Ford or Sears, Roebuck..." And even in the business field, the desire for money is but a symptom of the underlying drive to accomplish measurable results in risk-related tasks under one's own control.

Marketing use of motivation theory

Few areas in marketing have been studied as much as motivation. One of the perennial questions of marketing managers is, *What makes people buy?* They are complex creatures, and there is apparently no simple answer to this question. Also, the problem is further complicated by the fact that there are likely to be many motives operating on a person at any one time.

The several studies to which we now turn should make this clear. It should be kept in mind that some of the studies might well have been placed in a different category. As noted above, behavior is likely to be multi-motivated. In this sense, the classification is somewhat arbitrary. It is suggested that the reader exercise his or her own judgment as to the motivation involved in any particular case.

The motivating effects of dissonance

Obviously, as consumers we are constantly faced with choices. Sometimes we postpone a purchase and, of course, not all choices are of the same importance to us. Some are routine, some are of middling consequence, and some are of considerable consequence indeed.

An important aspect of many of these choices is that they are mutually exclusive. Usually, if we buy the black and white television, we forego the color set; if we purchase the Ford, we do not buy the Chevrolet. Yet prior to our choice, each of the alternatives looks attractive; each has pluses and minuses. Hence, if A is chosen over B, the qualities of B that initially prompted us to consider it seriously pulled in opposite directions from those of A. Doubt arises. We may say to ourselves: "I should have purchased the color TV set in the first place," or "The Chevrolet really has a better engine than the Ford," and so on. This type of post-decision dissonance motivates people to seek ways to reduce it. What consumers think after they make a selection can be quite important to marketing managers. Repeat customers are the lifeblood of a firm. Few companies could survive on new customers alone.

Brehm, in an early study of dissonance, asked a sample of women to rate the desirability of several products. They were given a choice between two of the items. After selecting an item, they were again asked to rate it. Hence, each product was rated for desirability before and after a choice. The women in their second rating, after the choice had been made, showed a tendency to increase their preference for the item selected and further decrease their desire for the item not chosen. And in a more recent study by LoSciuto and Perloff concerning the choice of a record album, the findings were in the same direction. The dissonance was reduced by re-evaluation of the item, giving greater desirability to the chosen record album, and assigning further undesirability to the one rejected.

These findings are in keeping with one of the ways theory suggests that dissonance may be reduced — upgrading the chosen item and downgrading the rejected item. The conclusions of LoSciuto and Perloff, however, were disputed in a later analysis by Oshikawa indicating that the ranking procedure used by LoSciuto and Perloff seriously biased the results. Apparently, further research is needed.

It will be recalled that another device suggested by theory to reduce dissonance is to seek post-decision information — information favorable to the choice made. The purchase of an automobile has been studied to examine this aspect of dissonance theory.

The purchase of an automobile is of considerable importance — there is ego involvement, and there are reasonably close substitutes on the market. After purchasing an automobile, post-purchase anxiety is likely to arise as one dwells on the good points of the car not purchased and which, of course, are now foregone, and on the weak points of the car actually purchased and whose weaknesses will now be present to plague the purchaser. Dissonance theory suggests the ways that anxiety can be reduced, among which is the option of buttressing or reinforcing the original thoughts that led to the purchase, as previously mentioned.

For example, studies show that people read the ads of products that have already purchased. A layman's view might be that advertisements are only meant to offer pre-buying information, not post-purchase assurance that a good decision has been made. An individual who originally considered buying a Ford or a Chevrolet and, after weighing the pros and cons of each make, purchased the Ford, now reads the Ford ads. Since the Ford ads are pro-Ford, anxiety is thereby reduced.

Engel, in his work on automobile buyers, did not find confirmation of this dissonance reduction process. Some dissonance, however, was noted in regard to price. While not disputing the possibility of the post-decision search for information to reduce dissonance or to increase dissonance which may magnify unhappiness to the point of action, Engel suggests that better tools of measurement are necessary to measure the commitment that must be present if cognitive dissonance is to be an element in the post-decision behavior.

It seems fairly obvious, then, that the subject of cognitive dissonance requires a word of caution. The generally critical review of the basic experiments on dissonance by Chapanis and Chapanis and the questions that arise from such studies as those of Engel and Oshikawa indicate that the value of the theory of cognitive dissonance to marketing is not yet firmly established.

Risk reductions and shopping behavior

Consumers quite naturally are motivated to make a purchase in order to attain some buying goal, and the method used is likely to be the one that promises the greatest certainty of getting exactly what is wanted with the greatest convenience possible. Donald Cox and Stuart Rich, in a study of telephone shopping, found that one of the strongest motives for shopping by phone was convenience, but the strongest deterrent was the fear of not getting what was wanted. Telephone shopping apparently seems too risky to many — almost two-thirds of the shoppers had not shopped by phone during the previous year. Those who did used risk-reducing techniques. In telephone shopping, risk can be reduced in at least two ways: by seeking more information or reducing what is at stake in the purchase. For example, women can limit telephone shopping to items where they know the brand, size, color, style, code number, and so on. They can telephone only to reorder what has already turned out previously to be satisfactory. They can seek more information by reading advertising or asking to talk to sales clerks, and so on. All of these aids can be furnished by the marketing manager — he can keep ads informative, make known styles, sizes, color, code numbers, brands, switch calls to shopping guides, see to it that goods are as advertised to encourage reorders, etc. There was some indication from the cases studied by Cox and Rich that costs associated with the above sales help might well be offset by the increased volume. Viewing pictures of goods on the Internet or in catalogs also helps reduce risk to customers.

Motivation and ego-bolstering needs

A study by Gerald Bell was concerned, among other things, with the methods used by individuals to protect themselves from being persuaded to make a purchase in instances where they lacked self-confidence. An individual may have self-confidence as to his own general handling of problems, yet not be confident in a specific case because of lack of experience or knowledge relevant to a given purchase. Of course, there are other possibilities — lack of general self-confidence, but strong self-confidence in a specific case where expertise is achieved and so on.

Bell found, among other things, that in car purchases those with high general self-confidence and low specific self-confidence were motivated to seek help in purchasing. Their general self-confidence apparently permitted them to acknowledge the lack of skill in buying specific products — in this case an automobile. "Purchase pals" were taken along to lend support and expertise.

Consumer purchases and self-image

It will be recalled that among the fundamental motives listed earlier were the needs for esteem, personal enhancement, and acceptance in the eyes of "important others." Both Maslow and Bayton spoke of motives that involve the concept of self-actualization. Several researchers have done studies in this area of the self-concept to determine how an individual seeks the support and esteem of others through the purchase of products.

Many items we buy communicate to others the kind of person we think we are or would like to be. Our interest in being well thought of and having others see us as we wish them to, means that our purchase of these ego-involved goods is made, to a considerable extent, with an eye to who else is buying them. We are concerned that they be people with whom we wish to be associated.

In a study designed to investigate the importance of the self-concept in brand/product selection, Grubb and Hupp studied the purchasers of two brands of automobiles — the Volkswagen 1200-1300 series and the Pontiac GTO series. Their hypothesis was: *Consumers of a specific brand of a product would hold self-concepts similar to the self-concepts they attribute to other consumers of the same brand. Further, consumers of a specific brand would hold self-concepts significantly different from self-concepts they attributed to consumers of a competing brand.*

Their findings tended to show rather clear stereotypes of the car owners involved. Volkswagen owners were described as thrifty, sensible, creative, individualistic, practical, conservative, economical, quality conscious. The Pontiac GTO owners, on the other hand, were seen as status-conscious, flashy, fashionable, adventurous, interested in the opposite sex, sporty, style-conscious, and pleasure-seeking.

The author's findings thus tended to confirm their hypothesis. Owners had concepts of themselves and of others who owned the same brand of product that were in congruence. They were, apparently, in the company of the people they wanted to be with, at least as they saw it.

73

Another study, in much the same vein, was done by Birdwell, who was also interested in the theory that much purchase behavior is a function of self-image and that choices are influenced by the way in which the individual wishes others to see him. Again, the motives involved are probably in the general area of the need for self-enhancement, esteem, and ego-defense. Birdwell's findings give considerable support to the notion that people select a product because it is "like them." This was especially true of the owners of group (1) cars — the Cadillac, Lincoln, and Mercedes owners — although the same finding applies to the other groups in varying degrees. Over the range of products this phenomenon may be generalized and will require further research.

PERCEPTION

The question of how we perceive things is by no means as simple as it would seem. Do things appear as they do because it could be no other way? Because that is how they are "out there" in space? No one really believes this because we have too many indications that it is false. Moving pictures do not really move; they are a series of stills. The rod in the glass of water is not really bent. The sun does not really go around the earth. The mountain is not really awesome or majestic. We just perceive or "see things" this way.

Of course, not all people experience things in the same manner. Even when presented with the same object or event, individuals often "see it" differently. The lumber entrepreneur or the highway planner sees the mountain quite differently than the artist or the nature lover. Each, because of personal interests and value structure, focuses on what for him or her are the relevant and salient features and ignores or treats as background the rest of the scene. The lumberman sees raw material, the highway planner sees a mound of dirt, the artist sees sunlight and shadows and masses of color. And even the same person, at different points in time, may perceive the same object or event in a "different light." Perception is selective, and intervening experience may alter the selection.

If this is the case, as it seems to be, can we say we perceive only what we wish to perceive? Do we see only what our interests dictate? Hardly; at least not in the extreme sense suggested by the question. The mountain, for example, is there for all to experience, as anyone trying to get to the other side will find out, yet in some manner we not only detect reality but at the same time construct and give meaning to it.

The question of how and what we perceive is, in part, also a matter of nerves and tissues. The stimuli that hit our sense organs are once removed from the objects that are their source, and what travels from the receptor sense organ to the brain is energy. Hence the problem of perception really is how energy is transformed into meaning.

The scope of perception

It should be noted at this point that perception is not confined to sight. We perceive things and events through all of the senses — touch, taste, smell, sight, and so on. Perception, in essence, is the process of linking the energy of all the excited sense organs to mental processes. A blind man has precepts — he knows reality in his own way of touch, sound, and other senses and can locate objects and understand their spatial relationships and uses.

Also, in the study of perception there has been much interest in the close relationship of perception to learning and cognition. One can readily move from studying the reception of simple sensations to an analysis of them as precepts and then move on to concept formation. Perception itself is usually defined as "sensory experience which has gained meaning." Perception lies somewhere between raw sensation and the more cognitive term "concept." In short, while perception has sensory data as its core, it in turn has a central role in the cognitive and thinking process. We are reminded again of the interrelationship among psychological processes.

We will proceed in this discussion with a discourse on the two main approaches outlined above. First, we will discuss briefly some of the work done by those who study primarily the mechanism, the limits, and the potentialities of our sensory system, especially the eyes. We will then turn to the points of view of those who emphasize the individual's part in translating the data of the senses into meaning and the manner in which interests, values, and personality needs are woven into the interpretation of sensations. The distinction between the two approaches should not be labored. It is a matter of emphasis. The physical structure of the sensory apparatus — i.e., the eyes, ears, nose, skin — is spelled out in all standard texts and will not be dealt with here. What is important for our purpose is to become acquainted with the limitations of the sensory mechanisms through which we turn raw sense data into meaning.

Perception and marketing management

The uncontrollable working of the eye is well known. The pupils dilate in response to light, darkness, fear, arousal, and so on. Various marketing studies show the nature of this predictable response and relate it to advertising, message reception, and the like.

Pupil dilation apparently occurs when stimuli are pleasant or when fear and anxiety are experienced. On the other hand, the pupils contract when stimuli lack the power to arouse interest. From this it is apparent that when there is reason to expect that people will not, or cannot, reveal their reaction to products or advertising, or when a check on verbal responses is desired, pupil measurement may help to get a more accurate response. Of course, the fact that pupils dilate both to pleasant stimuli and to fear stimuli makes it necessary that care be taken in research studies to control this variable.

In an article entitled *Looking Without Learning*, some interesting points were made relevant to perceptual processes. The eyes, when reading an advertisement, proceed in a scanning fashion over the page. The eyes rove about, occasionally "fixing" on specific spots and, as measured by a machine called the "optiscan," some individuals scan more than others. Apparently the more one scans, the more one learns. The interesting point in this study is the finding that some ads are written in such a way that they require more scanning to "get" the message than other ads. Efficient ads give up their meaning without undue burden in scanning. In short, to the extent that these findings can be generalized, communication is a shared task. However, we do not know too much about this phenomenon. Is eye movement related to the style of the ad, to the product advertised, to the brand? More research is required on this topic.

In another study the movement of the eyes as they read an advertisement indicated that individuals scan in a consistent pattern. Apparently, each individual has a pattern that is distinctive. What is of interest here is that the pattern of scanning apparently persists regardless of the size of the ad. Further, individuals differ substantially in the areas they scan and the degree to which an individual fixes or concentrates on a particular part of an ad appears unclearly related to "communication." The message received apparently has not much to do with the physical act of fixing on a particular part of the ad. Here, again, we need more studies before generalizations can be made.

Perception of time

Martilla and Thompson studied the perceived time duration of television commercials, particularly piggyback commercials, to determine whether or not two different 30-second commercials, back to back, are perceived as longer than a single 60-second commercial.

Using some 250 students and a university's closed television system, an experiment was conducted by employing a six-second Ford Mustang commercial sponsored by a local dealer, a 60-second food products commercial for a local supermarket, and a 30-second version of each of these placed back to back. A 60-second Bayer aspirin commercial was also shown. A 16-item questionnaire was used to gather reactions to the film.

Among other findings, the one that is important here is that "a 60-second two-product piggyback was perceived as lasting 25% to 30% longer than a single product commercial of the same length." The authors suggest precautions against generalizing from this experiment. The sample was of male college students, and they had differential familiarity with an interest in the products.

Selection perception

In a study of non-smokers, light smokers, moderate smokers, and heavy smokers, it was found that while only 55% of the non-smokers thought the link between cancer and smoking had been proved, 86% of the heavy smokers thought the link had not been adequately demonstrated. Put the other way around, about half the non-smokers believed cancer was linked to smoking but only 14% of the heavy smokers thought so. Perception theory would suggest that heavy smokers would selectively avoid exposure to information sources that might disturb their smoking habits too drastically. Such appears to be the case. For example, 32% of smokers were consistent readers of articles on health, including articles dealing with cancer, while 60% of non-smokers read literature of the same type.

LEARNING AND CONCEPT FORMATION

We have made the point in previous sections that the several segments of psychology — motivation, perception, learning, and so on — are so intrinsically related that it does violence to separate them for individual analysis. We have seen that perception has an extremely close relationship to learning, and, as far as learning itself is concerned, we shall find that drives and motives initiate and furnish the energy and direction to the learning process.

Despite the desirability of relating the various psychological processes to each other, most texts and many articles and monographs treat them apart, much as we have done so far. However, in this section on learning, certain aspects of cognition will be included. Learning is the process of building up the thinking apparatus.

The study of learning

What is the scientist trying to determine as she runs rats through water mazes to seek out the role of muscular sensations in learning behavior? As she uses pigeons to illustrate the essence of superstition? As she supplies wire and cotton figures to act as surrogate mothers to uncover the relation of nature to nurture? As she places wires in the brains of rats to locate reward centers? As she places fruit outside the cage of a chimpanzee to see how the animal will get at it? As she designs programs for a learning machine? The scientists involved in these experiments are trying to gain some understanding of the process of learning, to find out how learning takes place.

77

The basic problem in understanding the learning process is finding out how and under what conditions behavior is directed one way rather than another. An organism, whether non-verbal animal or verbal man, moves about in its environment and is rewarded or punished for its movements. Those acts that lead to better adjustment, i.e., more agreeable conditions, are repeated. Those that lead to maladaption, i.e., unpleasant situations, are avoided. In short, organisms are conditioned to the most rewarding survival pattern attainable at the time, all things considered.

We are here not so much interested in the fact of survival as we are in the process by which it is effected. How do we learn to survive? In some areas, of course, we have not learned. We have not learned how to avoid wars or crime. On the other hand, we have learned how to make war and how to commit crime. Possibly the underlying learning process is the same.

In any event, the analysis of learning is a process of breaking down a whole into its parts in order to determine how the parts contribute to the whole. As previously noted, sometimes the knowledge of the parts is difficult to add back to reproduce the whole. One senses that it is the relationship of the parts to each other that is important and that the whole is more than the sum of the parts. The field of learning, as we shall see, is split on this problem. Apparently it is not clear yet what parts to separate out or how to study the whole in order to arrive at a complete learning theory. At best, it appears that what is available are types of learning or learning principles of less than full generality. On the other hand, there appears to be a tendency to believe that, at bottom, there is but one learning process and all learning can be reduced to it.

Be that as it may, we find many explanations or schools of thought concerning the learning process. Possibly the basic reason for this diversity is that all we can observe is performance, the behavioral act. The nature of the process, what happens to bring this about, is inference. We observe a child cut himself on a sharp bottle. He stops handling the glass object. Later he avoids sharp cans, knives, and so on. We say he has learned to avoid "cutting objects." But how this generalization comes about we cannot literally see. Explanations for the fact of such new behavior are in conflict.

Without placing too much importance on the distinction, it can be said that there are two general orientations to research on the learning processes. One approach is essentially the stimulus-response (S-R) approach in one form or another. Units of rewarded responses are built up to explain more complex acts. Both classical and operant learning are basic representatives of this approach.

The other approach leans more toward types of cognitive processes and/or insight, or an approach that explains learning by the organism's ability to recognize relationships of parts to wholes not in step-by-step sequences but rather by a sort of structuring of the stimuli in the environment.

It should be stated at the outset that not all behavior is learned behavior. There are also unlearned responses to stimuli. It is an unlearned response to want to quench thirst, it is a learned response to desire Coca-Cola. In addition, some behavior changes are due to maturation. That part of behavior which is due to mere growing up should not be confused with behavior acquired by learning. Behavior possible for an adult may be out of the question from someone younger. Nor do individuals inherit or possess the same capacity or capabilities to perform.

Learning theory and marketing applications

Many marketing activities — advertising, package and product design, sales training, and selling campaigns, to name just a few — are designed and developed with the intent of persuading the consumer to purchase a product or service. Persuasion, however, implies thought processes, reasoning, learning, and remembering. In the attempts of marketing managers and researchers to understand the marketing process, studies have been designed to find out how learning takes place. How, for example, do people learn to like a product? How do they learn to switch brands? What goes on in their minds when they hear a TV program, read an advertisement, listen to a sales talk, or visit a store? Are they actively learning or passively reacting? Under what conditions do they act habitually and under what conditions do they learn to act in novel ways? The studies that follow will give some indication of learning theory in marketing analysis.

Learning without involvement

Herbert Krugman, in a study of TV commercials, questions the application of the usual learning process to the learning of television commercials. He makes a distinction between high-involvement product preferences where pros and cons are consciously examined and opinion and attitude change may take place before purchase, and the learning of material that is perceived as trivial or unimportant. Krugman cites the work on the learning of non-sense and low-involvement material by Ebbinghaus and Hovland. The point he makes is that in the case of TV commercials that are unimportant to an individual, the constant learning and forgetting of the commercials may operate to alter the cognitive salience of brands or products with the result that a potential change in the frame of reference is built up. This potential is "triggered" into overt behavior if and when the advertised product is purchased when it is seen in the store. The latent change in the perceptual structure, learned without conscious effort while listening repeatedly to TV commercials and the in-store display, are apparently each essential parts of this behavior pattern. If the purchase proves satisfactory, the consumer's attitude toward the product may shift to match the behavior. This is not a rationalization after the fact but the emergent response of the previously changed perception or frame of reference.

CONCEPT CATEGORIZING – NARROW AND WIDE

A recent laboratory study by Popielarz has to do, in part, with the breadth of categorizing. We have already referred to studies on breadth of categorization and noted that some individuals may be classified as broad categorizers — they have very wide tolerance as to what will fall into a class. Such individuals tend to overlook difference in objects and concentrate on likeness. They tend to assimilate. Then there are the narrow categorizers — individuals who tend to emphasize differences and overlook likeness. They tend to contrast rather than assimilate.

Popielarz hypothesized that wide categorizers would be more likely to purchase new products than would narrow conceptualizers. In his study using product cameras and employing both male and female subjects, he found support, althhough not overly strong, for this hypothesis. Breadth of categorization and willingness to try new products are related. Further research on other types of products and in actual purchase situations is needed before any generalizations can be hazarded in this area.

Concept generalization and brand choice

The use of concept generalization in studying the carryover of meaning from one product in a line of branded goods to another product in the line where all the products are physically different yet share a common brand is reported by Kerby. The psychological principle of generalization involved is that people have a tendency (1) to view two or more items as similar if they possess relatively similar physical characteristics, and (2) to view two or more stimuli as similar if they carry a common meaning even though differing in physical attributes.

In a laboratory experiment using photographs of four different products manufactured by a single firm and carrying a common brand name and, as control, four products similar but manufactured by eight different firms, Kerby found lack of evidence that such carryover is present. His limited study indicates that caution is called for with respect to semantic generalization. The "goodwill" associated with one product in a family of brands may not safely be assumed to "spill over" to other products in the line, in cases where the products are quite dissimilar, even though both are General Electric, Westinghouse, and so on.

Kerby suggests, among other qualifications, that semantic generalization may take place where less important products are involved rather than with "big-ticket" items. Here differences may be too great for likeness to be imputed across a company's line. Further research is required in this area before any underlying forces can be stated with assurance.

ATTITUDE

The study of attitudes seems to absorb a lion's share of the efforts of market researchers. There is apparently a constant need to know what people "think" — i.e., what their attitude is concerning new products, old products, brand names, prices, promotion campaigns, sales personnel, and so on. What is important in many cases is whether the attitudes are strong or weak, changing or stable, and the like. And it appears that this study of attitudes is in step with the times, as evidenced by the polls on attitudes and opinions regarding political candidates and on matters of public interest such as pollution control, ethnic relations, fluoridation, and education. In any event, problems in attitude theory and attitude measurement are under constant discussion and analysis.

Attitudes: What are they?

It should be mentioned at the outset that an attitude is not something that we can observe. We observe overt acts of behavior that are manifestations of what we impute to be an attitude. In this sense attitudes are constructs. And if, as we have seen, there is lack of precision in the definition and meaning of the concepts of learning, motivation, and perception, there is even more debate concerning the exact nature of attitudes.

Blumer, for example, apparently argues that there is no scientific basis for the concept. His point, it seems, is that there is no generic referent to which attitudes can lay claim. Individual attitude studies may be measuring something, but it is not rigorously established that what they are measuring is the same phenomenon.

Not many writers take such a dim view, however. DeFleur and Westie, for example, argue that there are, basically, two major conceptions of the nature of attitudes — probability conceptions and latent process conceptions. This dichotomy does not deny differences in the manner or weights given by various authors to the inclusion or exclusion in attitudinal models of motivational, perceptual, or cognitive elements. What they are saying, apparently, is that the general framework from which attitudes may be analyzed falls within one or the other of these approaches.

Without getting into too much detail, the probability approach means that attitudes are looked upon merely as the likelihood or chance that a certain opinion belief or course of action will recur in a given instance. For example, it is highly probable that the owner of a retail chain will persistently complain about a sales tax. This consistency in verbal behavior is the attitude. It is nothing more. Of course, this attitude may also be one of a cluster of beliefs regarding taxation; i.e., taxes on business are too high, tax revenues are squandered, government is too powerful, and so on. In any event, the point is that attitudes are merely observable behavior with a given probability of occurrence, given appropriate situations, and stimuli.

On the other hand, the latent process conception holds that there is more to an attitude than the behavioral response and its probability of occurrence. What precipitates or governs the persistent response we call an attitude is, for this school of thought, an intervening variable, a "hidden mechanism" that operates within the individual between the observable responses, verbal or otherwise, and the stimuli initiating the responses. Just how invariant responses are expected to be is not always clear.

Each of these approaches has its difficulties. In the first instance, where attitudes are defined as probabilities, it may quickly become tautological as an explanatory device. If an individual is observed more or less uniformly to reject the attitude stimulus, and we seek to explain this fact, it is not a legitimate answer simply to say "it is because he has a negative attitude." This would be, of course, completely tautological. The uniformity of his behavior cannot legitimately be used to explain itself.

The difficulty of the second method, which posits an inner mechanism, is that it is almost impossible to analyze an unobservable, inner entity.

The comparative merits of these two approaches, however, are not of importance here. What is important is that those using the term "attitude" be aware of the manner in which they are employing it and of the inferences they intend to make from the attitude in question. Apparently, as in the case of many of the constructs studied so far, i.e., social class, reference groups, motivation, learning, and so on, we use concepts that do not have universal acceptance but must be judged by how well they aid in understanding behavior.

CHAPTER 8
Managing the Product

A human being goes through life trying to satisfy unlimited wants and needs. He satisfies these wants and needs with the help of tangible entities. Hunger is satisfied by food that can be smelled, seen, tasted. Need for clothing is satisfied by clothing, apparel that can be seen, touched.

Beyond the basic need satisfaction, as seen in the buyer behavior, there are other things such as status, image, etc., that also need to be satisfied. They are often intangible in nature but do play a very important and vital role.

It is the need for status, image, etc., that will greatly influence the choice of a restaurant for consumer food. It is the same need that will influence the choice of a shop or choice of the label while choosing clothing apparel.

Thus, our needs and wants are partially satisfied by a tangible entity and partially by the intangibles attached to the tangible entity. This need-satisfying entity is known as a *Product*. It is the first and the most important of the 4Ps of marketing.

➤ Without the product there is noting to attach a price tag to.
➤ Without the product there is nothing to package.
➤ Without the product there is nothing to distribute.
➤ Without the product there is nothing to promote.
➤ Which is to say that without the product there is no marketing.

There are utility aspects to the *Product*, for example, product features that help give a benefit. Then there are non-utility aspects to the *Products*, for example, packaging, brand name, etc.

Both put together build the personality of the *Product*, which is a *Total Product Offering*. This *Total Product Offering* is what helps the buyer in attaching the "value" to the product on the basis of the buyer's perception of the abilities of the *Total Product Offering* to satisfy wants and needs.

The Personality of the product is made up of five components:

1. The core or the basic constituent
2. The associated features
3. The brand name
4. The package
5. The label

We shall discuss them one by one.

THE CORE OR BASIC COMPONENT

It is the most important component of the product personality. If the core component itself is bad, then no amount of promotion and addition of other features can make the product survive. For example, Close-up Toothpaste is the product that gives the user a fresh feeling, by virtue of the mouthwash. It has a unique taste and is promoted as a product for the younger generation, giving confidence to the user while interacting with the opposite sex.

The core component here is the toothpaste. If the toothpaste does not help in basic existence, no amount of personality can help.

The features

Carrying the same Close-up example further, the mouthwash is a feature of the product. It is around this feature that the product personality is often built.

Brand name

Brand is a marketing term. It means name, term, symbol, or design, or a combination of these which is intended to identify the goods and services of one seller or group of sellers and to differentiate it from those of the competitors. A brand name is a major component of the personality. It also facilitates advertising and promotion. The marketers promote the brands aggressively and make the customers brand-conscious. Thus, the consumer does not ask simply for a bath soap, but asks for Ivory.

Packaging

Apart from protecting the product, the packaging also serves another important function, that of adding aesthetics appeal to the product and making it distinctively different than the others. The packaging material, color scheme, size, aesthetics, and other feature elements exert a lot of influence on the sale of the product. When packaging is changed, the product is advertised as if it were new to attract new consumers.

Labeling

The label helps a buyer in understanding more about the product by giving him information about features, uses, etc.

Product policy

Broadly, the product policy involves:

➤ Appraisal of the product line and the individual products

- Decisions on product differentiation
- Product positioning
- Brand decisions
- Decisions on packaging
- New product development

Product line and product appraisal

All products have a limited lifespan for various reasons. However, in order to prolong the life of the product, the marketer has to keep a close watch on the happenings surrounding that product. One way of doing this is by continually appraising the quality, profitability, and appeal of the product and comparing it with lead to withdrawal of the product, change in advertising, etc. The product may have various models having differing specifications, otherwise known as product mix.

It may so happen that one model may eat into the sale of the other. Such conflicts within the product line have to be resolved. The decisions referred to here form part of the product policy.

Product differentiation

Day by day the brands are becoming similar because technology is no longer a prerogative of a chosen few. When there is absolute similarity, the marketer has to give different reasons to the buyer to buy his product. This exercise is known as *Product Differentiation*. The purpose of differentiation is to:

- help create different identity
- generate brand loyalty
- endow product with real or imaginary psychological differences
- compete on different price levels
- locate attributes that will generate differential responses
- create product position

Product pricing

Pricing not only affects profits but can also affect the image of the product and the company. It is usually believed that high price means high quality and low price means low quality, and yet messages like "Bargain Offers," "Never Before Prices," Clearance Sale," attract buyers in large numbers. Everybody wants value for money. Each buyer has an equation of money and value which is exclusively his or her own and is based on various factors. The buyer's rejection of the product because of its price need not necessarily mean he or she cannot afford it. In his equation of cost-benefit, the costs may outweigh the benefits.

Price also has other psychological impacts, e.g., a price of $1.99 appears less expensive than if it were $2.00. Many manufacturers and retailers have used such a pricing policy successfully for many years.

The manner in which price reduction is projected also has different effects. What sounds better . . .

➤ 10% discount, or
➤ Save $10

. . . for a product otherwise costing $100?

➤ If the same product were to be offered at $92 with a message, "Save almost 10%"?

It has been found that people are attracted more towards the idea of saving and, therefore, discounts, etc., should be promoted accordingly.

Price can be and is used tactically to steal an edge over competition.

There are four approaches to pricing:

COST BASED

Cost-based pricing is based on the total cost of the product including cost of production and overhead. To these, a predetermined percentage of profit margin is added and the total is offered as selling price.

Limitations: The cost is calculated on the basis of certain predetermined levels of demand. The demand may fluctuate due to various factors beyond control and, therefore, this method of pricing may not be adequate. However, this approach helps indicate minimum price levels.

DEMAND BASED

This approach explores the effect of different prices on the demand of the product. On the basis of different selling prices and varying production volumes, the breakeven point is calculated. This approach highlights the impact of price on volume and price to arrive at the optimum price / volume ratio.

Advantage: If the demand for the product is a function of price, then this approach is realistic.

Limitation: It is difficult to predict with accuracy the impact of price variation on demand.

COMPETITION BASED

The product can be priced in a number of ways.

➤ Above competitors' prices
➤ Below competitors' prices
➤ Same as competitors' prices

MARKET BASED

As discussed earlier, every buyer has a price:value equation in his or her own mind which is unique not only to the commodity, but also to the individual. Whenever the buyer considers that value satisfaction that the commodity delivers, it is the perceived value. Such perceived value can be the outcome of:

➤ Value for money as influenced by all aspects of the firm, its product, and its services. For example, Maytag products attract higher price because of a very conscious effort on the part of the company to promote itself as a manufacturer of high quality and reliable products.
➤ Endorsements by socially renowned people or exclusivity of a product as perceived by the buyer or . that appeals to the "image" that the buyer identifies will also affect perceived value.
➤ Certain market segments may attach certain value to the product performance.
➤ Price barriers that are apparent in different segments.

It is essential to accurately assess a market's perception of the value of a product. This is where market research can be of great help. The seller may hold an inflated view of the product value. This may result in overpricing. On the part of the buyer, price:value is a qualitative judgment based on the buyer's experience of the competition. Well administered research can avoid the danger of overpricing. Conversely, the seller may conservatively assess the value of his product, resulting in underpricing. This too can be avoided by market research.

STRATEGIES OF PRICING

Though a function of corporate and company objectives, locating the price of the product within the given acceptable price range is always a tough decision to make. The pricing decision is influenced by:

➤ the objective of return on investment
➤ targeted market share
➤ competition
➤ profit objective
➤ need to stabilize the prices

Pricing can be arrived at by following various approaches such as those summarized below.

Skimming price policy: The price is set at the top of the acceptable price range. If administered for pricing the product in the early stages of its life cycle, it can help in recovering investments.

This approach tries to neutralize the probability of pricing mistakes that may result in pricing the product low.

High price can also help in segmenting the market, as well as to strategically limit the volume of sales, especially when production capacity and or stocks are inadequate.

Higher price, though, often results in low volumes that may result in underutilization of production capacity. Similarly, high price will limit induction of trial in consumers, resulting in acceptance at a low rate. This result in the early stages can be damaging.

Penetration pricing: As opposed to the earlier approach, penetration pricing resorts to gaining maximum market penetration in a short span of time. Therefore, a low price is set in the hope of attracting high volume.

High volume results in economy of scale, while in the process winning a wide product acceptance.

Low price means low profits meaning longer payback periods. This can be disastrous if the product has a very short life cycle. Low price could achieve desired market penetration, but if the company is compelled to raise the prices over a period of time it may face resistance.

Marginal pricing: The objective in setting a price is that it must be low enough to attract and retain the maximum number of buyers and should also be such that it earns decent profits for the company. One of the approaches taken to arrive at the sensible price is known as *Marginal Costing*. It simply means *the cost of producing one more piece*.

To arrive at the cost for producing one more unit it is presumed that the volumes necessary to pay for the fixed costs already exist. This further implies that the cost for producing more units are variable costs. This approach ensures additional contribution to profits. Generating this type of business, however, results in reduction in return on sales and, therefore, low profit. In the long run, the approach could be suicidal. However, faced with an option of accepting or rejecting an order, marginal costing may result in a price that is low enough to get the order and high enough to ensure some contribution to profit. This approach is often used when the price is elastic, the product volumes are high, and high sales volumes are decisive to the business.

SUMMARY

The buyer does not seek cheap product, but is interested in the product that is economical. The buyer wants the maximum number of benefits at an optimum price. These benefits are not related to product utility alone, but are also a function of image.

Though price plays an important role in purchase decisions, it is not a singularly important factor. While resorting to competitive pricing strategy, it is necessary to ensure the authenticity of facts. This can avoid pricing blunders resulting in a detour from the objective.

While preparing a marketing plan, due importance should be given to costs, margins, and prices. The plan should also include the competitors' pricing. Preferably, pricing considerations and options based on competitive information and research findings should also be included in the plan.

A typical price setting process:

1. To begin with, establish marketing objectives. They could be:
   - profit maximization
   - increase in market share
   - quality, leadership
2. Access elasticity of demand and determine probable quantity purchased at alternative price levels.
3. Estimate costs at varying output levels.
4. Examine competitors' prices.
5. Select pricing method.
6. Select the final price, express it effectively, and ensure that it is acceptable to the company sales force as well as the participants in distribution channels.

CHAPTER 9
New Product Development

Market conditions are dynamic in nature. Therefore, a decision made today may not prove to be adequate tomorrow. Thus, product policy devised and implemented presently may fall short on meeting the forthcoming changes. This necessitates the effort for developing new products, and new product development forms a vital part of product policy. The need for new product development can be attributed to:

➤ Meeting changes in demand
➤ Enhancing profits
➤ Adopting to changing environment
➤ Combating environmental threats

MEANING OF NEW PRODUCT

The organization may develop new products because of:

➤ Technological innovations
➤ Marketing oriented modifications

Technological innovations will lead to new functional utilities, whereas marketing oriented innovations are initiated by the marketing department of the organization. Such changes initiated by the marketing department on the basis of feedback from the market could be:

➤ Change in color
➤ Change in packaging
➤ Change in brand name
➤ Change in product position

STAGES IN NEW PRODUCT DEVELOPMENT

New product development does not result from a stroke of luck, neither does it take a genius to do it. It is a well conceived, controlled, and coordinated effort. The effort progresses through five distinct stages.

1. Generating ideas
2. Screening ideas
3. Concept testing

4. Business analysis and market analysis
5. Product development test marketing and commercializing

Generating ideas

The new product ideas are contributed to by many players:

➤ Customers
➤ Distributors and wholesalers
➤ Company personnel
➤ Research organizations

Studying the problems faced by the customer with the existing product is often found to be a logical point of beginning. Creativity techniques such as brainstorming are also used by putting together a group of people and encouraging them to air their views.

Screening

Mere generation of the idea is not enough, it has to be evaluated. This is done by asking questions such as:

➤ Is there a felt need for the new product?
➤ Is it an improvement over an existing product?
➤ Is it close to our current line of business?
➤ Does it take us to a totally new line of business?
➤ Can the existing marketing organization handle the product?
➤ Or does it need extra expertise on the production and marketing front?

The more attractive looking ideas pass on to the product concept testing stage. The list is by no means exhaustive.

Testing

Done to ascertain the perception of the consumer as well as to crystallize the idea for the organization, concept testing takes the exercise of new product development a long way. By using quantitative techniques, an effort is made to understand the customer's perception of the product vis-à-vis certain product attributes.

Business and market share analysis

This is the stage in which the vital business decisions are taken and analyzed. The project is evaluated from financial as well as from the business point of view. To make good decisions, the following information is necessary:

- Estimated demand
- Seasonal consumption patterns
- Competition
- Major competitors, their market share, the dominant market segments held by them
- Special market features affecting demand
- Price elasticity of demand
- Volume – cost-profit analysis at different feasible levels
- The nature of the marketing channel required, the nature of channels available, comparative costs/advantages of alternate channel types
- The marketing organization required for marketing the product; whether existing marketing organization can take care of the product or whether a new organization setup is required— if so, what would it cost to set up a new organization to market the product?

Development, test marketing, commercialization

Test marketing is undertaken to avoid costly errors. The exercise is undertaken with minimum possible cost or risk. It is a controlled exercise, and, on the basis of its results, the organization will make a decision to commercialize. Great care has to be taken in selecting, controlling, analyzing, monitoring the markets, and interpreting the results.

Demand estimation for new products

Demand estimation is the most critical factor in the new product development decision. Usually one of the following methods is used:

- Method of substitution/replacement
- End use method
- Market tests

Method of substitution replacement

A new product will usually replace an old one. Toothpaste replaced tooth powder. Nylon replaced cotton. By using standard forecasting methods, the demand for the existing product is first estimated, and potential demand for the new product is projected. It serves only as an upper limit, and research provides the help to develop a realistic estimate.

End use method

This method is used when a new product cannot be compared with the one that it is going to replace. The first method falls short when end use of the product is determined and the market categorizes and quantifies on the basis of end uses of the product. This, too, gives an upper limit of the estimated demand. Too narrow or too broad need identifications can be misleading.

Test marketing

It is probably the most reliable technique and has been discussed in detail in an earlier chapter.

CHAPTER 10
Product Life Cycle

Products, like living beings, have a certain span of life. This is known as the product life cycle, which is to say that:

➤ Products have a limited life.
➤ Profits from the product rise and fall at different stages of the life cycle.
➤ Products require different strategies at different stages in the life cycle.

As the diagram below illustrates, the life cycle has four distinct stages:

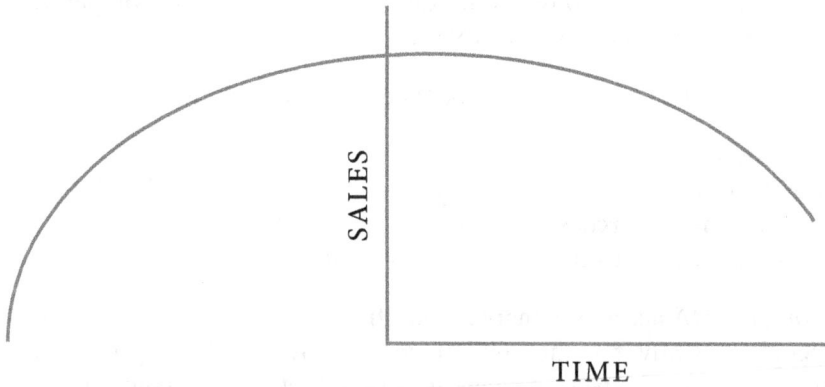

➤ Introduction
➤ Growth
➤ Maturity
➤ Decline

The beginning and the end of each stage are arbitrary.

Introduction stage

This is a period of slow growth, and profits may be non-existent because of heavy promotional expenses.

Growth stage

During this period the product acceptance increases rapidly, thereby improving the profits.

Maturity stage

Beyond a certain point of growth, the rate of growth declines due to acceptance of the product by a majority of potential buyers. The profits are at their highest in this period and start to decline because of sustenance of the product position against competitors, which demands high outlays.

Decline stage

During this stage, the sales nosedive, having a telltale effect on profits. Not all products pass through this curve of product life cycle — some may rise to maturity very quickly, some may achieve growth again after maturity.

A number of times it is the technology that makes the product obsolete. The winding wristwatch was made obsolete by quartz technology. The companies who adapt to changing technology can survive.

Acceptance of the product by the buyer is based on an AIDA model:

➤ Awareness about the product
➤ Interest in the product
➤ Desire to consume or purchase a product
➤ Action taken towards consumption or purchase of the product

Progress through AIDA across the market takes time. In the introductory stage only a few people may buy it — they are known as innovators. If the product is good, a larger number of buyers, known as early adoptees, will come to the product. Entry of competitors at this stage may speed up the adoption process by increasing product awareness. Subsequently, more buyers will use a product resulting in early majority. This means the product has gained reasonable acceptance and is now in the maturity stage as the number of potential buyers approaches zero. At this stage, the maximum purchases are replacement purchases. Beyond this point, new products may come into the market or interest of the buyer may be diverted elsewhere. The product now approaches the decline stage.

The ability of the marketer to innovate will determine the period through which the product will remain in the marketplace. To give the buyer new and different reasons to buy may result in product development, market development, suggestion of more usage per occasion and/or suggestion of different occasions for usage. For example, Bournvita is a drink traditionally promoted as a breakfast drink. A few years ago, Bournvita also tried to promote itself as a good night time drink. The long life of a product is obvious evidence of innovative marketing.

Depending upon the stage of the product in its life cycle, the strategies have to be adapted to maximize the outcome from the marketing environment. Here it is necessary to make a differentiation between *Product* and *Brand*. Often the words are used interchangeably.

By product, we mean a commodity or a gadget or a service being introduced to the market for the first time, i.e., the videocassette player is a product and color television is a product, whereas a Panasonic VCR is a brand and Zenith TV is a brand. The concept of the *Product Life Cycle* refers to the product and not a brand. Having identified the four distinct stages in the life of the product, let us now try to understand the strategies that may be adopted to maximize profit and at the same time increase the life span of the product.

STRATEGIES FOR THE INTRODUCTION STAGE

In the *Introduction Stage*, the strategy is determined on the basis of:

➤ Awareness about the product in the minds of the consumer
➤ The size of the market

No product awareness

In this situation the organization can price the product higher but support the product introduction with heavy promotion. This strategy, when there is no product awareness: HIGH PRICE + HIGH PROMOTION.

High promotion helps in creating awareness in the market.

At the same time, a HIGH PRICE attracts the adventurous buyers. They are buying the product before anyone else has, and by paying a higher price, they are gaining the feeling of exclusivity, while at the same time having the ability to pay the high price does a lot to their esteem needs.

Product awareness is high, but the market is limited.

At these times, too, organizations can choose to keep the price higher in view of the limited size of the market. Higher prices give an opportunity of recovering the costs faster. As the market is limited, it may not be necessary to indulge in a high promotion effort.

No product awareness and large market.

The larger the size of the market, the more the chances of competition entering quickly. To counter this possibility, it is advisable to ensure that your product reaches more and more consumers. This can be achieved by HEAVY PROMO-TION coupled with a low price.

High product awareness and large market.

The purpose of promotion is to make people aware of the product. A high degree of awareness means that the promotion may be low, and to enter into the marketplace and make it difficult for the competition to come in with a new brand, it is worthwhile to keep the price low.

STRATEGIES FOR THE GROWTH STAGE

This is a time when more people have become aware about the product and have understood about benefits that it can offer. At the same time, their expectations from the product vary.

➤ They may think that the price is too high or too low.
➤ Certain features may be found excessive or some found to be lacking.
➤ The distribution channel may not be effective enough to cater to the growing needs of the product.

This is the time when the organization can consolidate the effort by:

➤ Improving quality of the product
➤ Add/delete/modify features of the product
➤ Enter new market segments
➤ Create new distribution channels
➤ Reduce the price

STRATEGIES FOR THE MATURITY STAGE

The term maturity and its illustration in the *Product Life Cycle* diagram suggest stagnation. However, this is not the case. In reality, there is growth in product sale value by virtue of inflation. Also, there is a growth in the sales volume by virtue of market forces. However, this growth is steady over a period, meaning that if a certain market is growing at the rate of 15% each year, the sale of the product also grows at the same rate. The reason for maturity is usually the saturation of the distribution channels. The existing channels of distribution can no longer absorb larger quantities. The maturity could be a stable maturity, meaning no increase or decrease in sale. Or maturity could be a declining maturity, meaning a decline in sales each year.

STRATEGIES

The best strategy is the strategy of *Market Modification*. This can be achieved by:

Convert the non-users of the product to users

A certain cable TV operator had done this in an interesting way. She affiliated with a popular aerobics exercise class, recorded the classroom sessions, and offered them to her clients in their homes. Now the students need not attend class and can stay home and still obtain the benefits of aerobic exercise.

Enter new markets

A clock manufacturer, who began selling clocks as a timekeeping device, has started promoting its product as an ideal gift, personal or corporate, thus entering the gift item market.

Win competitors' customers – suggest frequent use

Tea is traditionally consumed as a morning drink with breakfast in some countries. The tea industry may be able to expand sales by promoting tea as a good night time drink.

More usage per occasion

Soft drinks have often been promoted as a family drink. A few years ago soft drink bottlers started promoting soft drinks as an ideal party drink as well, necessitating more use.

New uses

A milk substitute started as a whitener for tea or coffee. Later it could be promoted as a sweetener, and now it is being promoted as an ideal dessert maker.

Product modification

Adding new features to the product has its own benefits, such as:

➤ Quick adoption by non-users.
➤ People perceiving the organization as a progressive company.
➤ If modifications are promoted properly, they can bring in a lot of free publicity.
➤ It generates a lot of enthusiasm in sale and distribution personnel.

Market modification

This can be achieved by:

- ➤ Modification in price
- ➤ Modification in distribution channels
- ➤ Modification in advertising
- ➤ Modification in product promotion
- ➤ Modification in selling effort
- ➤ Modification in services

An innovative marketer can prolong the maturity of the product and can even push it to growth, ensuring better profits for the organization.

CHAPTER 11
Product Distribution

We have already discussed the 4Ps of marketing, which are:

➤ Product
➤ Price
➤ Promotion
➤ Place

No matter how well designed the product — keeping in mind the buyer and all the buyer's expectations of benefits — no matter how attractively priced it is, whether it fits any value for money or cost benefit equation that the customer has in mind, no matter how creatively the product is promoted with excellent offers that appeal to the customer, if the product is not made available to the customer at a place convenient to the buyer, all the exercises of *Product, Price,* and *Promotion* are done in futility.

This is what product distribution is all about. Depending upon the nature of the product and policy of the company, the channel of distribution must be decided. Particularly in the case of consumer products, the distance between consumer and the company could be large. The number of consumers, potential and loyal, is so large that it is physically impossible to reach each consumer directly to offer the product. Therefore, intermediaries are necessary. They can be wholesalers, distributors, or retailers.

Sometimes, the company may choose to bypass the retailers altogether and approach the customers directly through mail order. Automatic teller machines, or ATMs, being installed by banks is one example. Bottlers offering soft drinks through vending machines is another. Many companies using the Internet also follow this approach.

The company's decision of the marketing channel greatly affects all other marketing decisions. It has a bearing on price, advertising, size of sales force to be deployed, the need for training, the need for service setup, etc. One thing to understand here is that the channel decision involves a long-term commitment to other firms.

The product distribution system is a key external resource. It takes a long time to build and cannot be easily changed. In spite of the complexities and commitments involved, there are a number of good reasons that make distribution a worthwhile element of the marketing mix.

- The distribution intermediaries offer a ready-made network of contacts. Developing them afresh is a mammoth task and can take a very long time.
- Especially in the case of consumer products and consumer durables, distributors can offer a wide choice. Whenever products need to be compared, it can be easily done at the local retail shop.
- As the retailer or a distributor is dealing in a variety of products, the cost of stocking and selling can be spread over a number of items. Thus, the distributor can distribute the product at a lower cost than the company.
- The distributors often pay for the goods and stock the material. In a sense, they share the risk of investment.
- Distributors have a special knowledge of retailing and distribution that the company may lack.
- Presence of a distributor in a given area makes it economical for the company to operate, as it does not have to employ more sales persons to cover the area.

However, there are limitations.

- Distributors sometimes lack the level of commitment. As we saw in organizational buying behavior, their main purpose is to earn a profit. They will, by selling whichever product gives them profits.
- They expect the manufacturer to stimulate the demand for the product by advertising, etc.
- The decision of dealing with the customer directly or otherwise is dependent upon the availability of the suitable marketing channels. The disadvantage of being away from the customer and therefore exercising less control over sales has to be balanced by the economy of selling and servicing costs.

CHOICE OF DISTRIBUTION CHANNELS

The choice of the channels of distribution depends upon the following factors:

- Geographically dispersed customers. At such times, it becomes uneconomical to reach every customer. Local assistance in the form of dealers or distributors is useful.
- When the number of customers is large, and they buy in small quantities at a time.
- The bulkier the product, the higher the cost of handling. At such times, the transportation distance needs to be reduced, as well as the amount of handling. The products that need after sales service are usually sold through sole selling agents that are trained and qualified to maintain the required service standards. Similarly, the products that have a long order materializa-

tion period, such as industrial products — typically capital goods — can be sold through both direct selling and local selling agents.

➤ Whenever it is important to maintain inventory at a low cost, distributors come in very handy.
➤ The greatest influence is that of the competition. If the competitor's product is available to the customer through a certain channel the new entrant to the market is forced to follow.
➤ The goodwill that the company enjoys in the market, as well as the company philosophy and policy decisions also determine the choice of a channel. Sometimes companies choose to make a distinction between the types of customers they want to serve and the channel to be used. For example, in the computer industry, the company may operate in a city through its branch office as well as local dealers.
➤ Corporate clients, where the requirements are large and sometimes specialized, are handled directly by the local branch. The one-time users as well as first-time users are left to the dealers. Similarly, the company may choose to retain the service function, as it is most vital for the goodwill of the organization.
➤ As discussed elsewhere, companies sometimes have chosen to bypass the distributor even though their product falls in the category of consumer durables. They choose to approach the client directly even though the clients are large in number and also geographically dispersed.
➤ The environment also plays an important role in the channel decisions. The legal aspects may have a detrimental impact on sole distributor appointment. In case of depressed market conditions, the company may choose to economize on costs and therefore may choose to short-circuit some levels of distribution.

Channel management

For all practical purposes, the distributor or the agent or the wholesaler are direct extensions of the company they represent. Over and above, they also have their own ideas. Therefore, a good working relationship is essential. Both the company and the distributor have chosen to come together for mutual benefit. Therefore, it is a partnership of sorts and, like any other relationship, must be given time to develop.

Typically there are two types of middlemen, besides dealers/retailers:

➤ Distributors/wholesalers
➤ Selling agents

Distributors or wholesalers stock the product for the company and provide the necessary transportation infrastructure. The company may have its own sales force who will appoint the retailers, collect the orders, and follow up. Distributors/wholesalers will not only have the infrastructure for stocking the products, but will also provide an infrastructure for sales. They will appoint retailers and promote the product.

The distributors buy the product from the company and also invest in the infrastructure. The purpose is to motivate them to sell because they need to recover the investment they have made. It may also stop them from considering competing products.

The selling agent usually does not buy and sell. The agent books orders on behalf of the company and earns a commission. This capital is not at risk, therefore the agent's effort may be diluted to a considerable extent. Therefore, it is necessary to reach a proper agreement about duties and responsibilities of each party involved.

MOTIVATING THE DISTRIBUTOR/WHOLESALER

Though the terms and conditions, such as discounts and exclusivity, etc., could be motivation enough, it is necessary to continuously supervise and encourage. Therefore, the company has to sell through the distributors but also has to sell to the distributor.

Here, again, we have to start from the basics — to understand the needs and wants of the customer. Manufacturers usually take the view that the distributors neglect certain types of customers; their sales people lack necessary quality, they misuse the advertising material, etc. But this is a limited view. The important thing to remember here is that distributors/wholesalers are not "hired." They are customers in their own right. They have their own ideas and will look for opportunities to implement them. The distributors are in a peculiar position. Apart from being selling agents for the company, they also act as purchasing agents for the customer. Therefore, the distributor will sell any product that the customer wants to buy from the distributor.

The distributor is interested in selling an assortment of products, that way he or she can sell a combination to the customer. Therefore, the distributor may not direct all his resources, monetary or otherwise, towards a single product or brand. To gain the cooperation of the distributor, a number of times the carrot and stick approach is used. High discounts, special offers, and shared advertisement costs are expected to work as motivators, whereas threats to terminate relationships and penalty clauses are also expected to work as motivators.

This approach overlooks the needs, problems, strengths, and weaknesses of the distributor.

A longer lasting and a little more positive approach is that of partnership. The company forges a long-term relationship with the distributor. The responsibilities of each party are made explicitly clear. The commissions may be based upon their adhering to the policy.

The most disciplined approach is to establish a *distributor relations department*. This department identifies the needs of the distributor, builds a suitable program, and helps the distributor operate as optimally as possible. Along with the distributors, they will plan the objectives, inventory levels, advertising and promotional plans, training requirements, etc.

EVALUATION

The evaluation of performance should be done on the basis of set standards. These standards might include:

➤ Achievement of sales targets
➤ Stock levels
➤ Cooperation in company's promotional programs
➤ Customer (retailer) feedback on service

Overseas markets: Currently, exports are often important to a company. All elements of marketing apply overseas as well. The only difference in national marketing and overseas marketing is the distance between the seller and the buyer. This distance makes it necessary to involve the wholesaler of agents. Moreover, wholesalers often become very significant in this case because from country to country, language, culture, consumption patterns, etc., change. Besides, the local person or company often better understands the law that prevails in that land.

Certain products can be manufactured in one country and sold in another, without making any modifications, whereas certain products need to be modified according to local needs. The local distributor can be of great help in identifying such issues. Moreover, country to country, the practice of negotiations and business ethics may be different. Brand names, too, could need careful checking. There is the often-used example of a car named Nova, very popular in the United States, that would not sell in Mexico because in the local language Nova meant *No Go* — who would want or buy the car that does not go?

To sum up, the physical distribution activities could include:

➤ distribution communication
➤ demand forecasting with help of distributors
➤ inventory control

- order processing
- warehouse selection and maintenance
- return goods handling
- scrap salvage
- transportation
- storage

Each process between order receipt to order execution and delivery to customer must be kept under control. To work through any channel by implementing any method needs a clearly laid down policy and an effective communication and implementation of that policy.

CHAPTER 12
Internet and New Media Marketing

The internet and other new media are very useful to the executive in marketing today. An executive starting a new business or one working in an existing business today should examine the business products and services available on the internet to help the business person succeed in marketing.

One area to be investigated is internet technology. Virtually every business today needs to have access to the internet. The business person needs to explore the internet to help decide on an internet service provider and internet home office applications. Web hosting should be examined to determine the equipment and servers needed. Every business needs to have a web site which needs to be designed to meet the marketing and other internet communication needs of the firm. The URL needs to be registered, and the web site needs to be made available online to potential customers and others interested in the firm.

Possible internet services in communications need to be examined to develop voice messaging, online faxing, internet call waiting and call forwarding and other communication services. Choices of telephone services have been enhanced by the internet, and the firm can choose from traditional telephone service providers as well as newer providers of such services using the internet to supplement or replace standard telephone services. Information on office and cell phones and installation of telephone services can be accessed readily on the internet.

One interesting innovation that can be used with a computer is MagicJack. MagicJack is an adapter that plugs into a UBS port on your computer. It is a socket in which you can then plug in a regular telephone. MagicJack then provides a US phone number that can be used anywhere in the world. This service enables making calls to and from persons wherever they are located, usually at local calling rates. As of this writing the annual flat-rate fee charged by MagicJack for itnernet calling is $19.95 per year. Please see www.magicjack.com for more information on this service.

Another new technology for telephone service uses VoIP- "Voice over Internet Protocol". This technology lets you talk over the internet. Some products using VoIP require your computer to be turned on for use of this phone service which provides a virtual phone interface to the internet. You can talk to other subscribers of the same service with no telephone fees. You can dial the other number with clicks of your computer mouse, speak through a microphone, and listen through either speakers or a headset. One of the leading companies in this type of communications is Skype. Skype users can talk to other Skype users anywhere in the world for free and pay a small fee of (2.1 cents) to call a landline telephone in the United States, Canada and some other countries. You can also use video calling on Skype where you can actually see the person you are calling live on a video screen at no additional cost.

The simplest way to get started with Skype or a similar service is to use a laptop computer with an integrated camera and microphone or plug in to a USB port with a web camera with an integrated microphone. www.Skype.com will provide directions to connect your computer with their telephone service. This service is easy to use when you connect to other subscribers. To also be able to connect with landline telephones it is necessary to sign up for a monthly plan or pay as you go plan with Skype. Skype also offers a standalone videophone service.

Another option is to use a service like Vonage which enables you to connect your phone to other regular phones without leaving your computer on. This service requires a monthly contract. See www.vonage.com for more information on this option. See www.voipreview.org for a list of providers of similar services.

There is a variety of business software to help in business planning, accounting, web design, and general small business needs that can be utilized by new businesses and existing businesses as well. For example, business plans for new businesses and business plans for expanding existing businesses can be developed using internet software that aids in developing a business plan with financial projections to help the business gain investors or loans for development of the new business or existing business that wishes to expand its services.

There is a lot of information on the internet on starting, buying, or selling a company as well as information on buying a franchise. Leading internet service providers can easily be accessed over the internet.

Many specific services and processes that may benefit businesses are available on the internet. Some of these services can easily be accessed on the internet by using a source such as www.smammbizmanager.com or by a Google or other search on the internet. For example, when a business person needs to make arrangements for business travel such services as travel agencies, airlines, hotels, car rentals, currency information and weather information can easily be accessed over the internet.

The internet can provide information on staffing and recruiting of employees, can help by posting available jobs, can provide information on office temporary workers and agents, consultants and contractors. Employee services such as outsourcing of marketing services and other services, employee benefits, payroll, retirement plans, and health insurance are also available on the internet.

Other services such as shipping and marketing, legal services including incorporation and trademark and other legal areas, as well as tax information are many forms useful in marketing are also available on the internet.

Software retailers such as MicroWarehouse, Beyond.Com, Egghead, Amazon and Buy.com can also provide business software to aid businesses in marketing and other areas of business. Operating systems can be provided by companies such as Microsoft, Apple, eLinux and Redhat to provide business systems solutions and open systems solutions.

Used equipment can often be purchased through online auctions such as eBay auctions and other online auction services.

Financial services including small and large business banking, online banks, rate comparisons, insurance information, loan information, Small Business Administration loans, credit cards and credit checks and services are all available on the internet. Business Plan software is also available through Business Plan Pro and other services to help provide the information needed to help the business person support requests to prospective sources of capital for new, small and larger businesses.

Another useful tool to marketers is permission based, online direct marketing. This can be a powerful tool to reach very targeted audiences with messages. There are internet providers both for buying opt-in email lists based upon target markets or for outsourcing the entire direct marketing process.

Marketers for small companies especially also need to learn low to write direct email copy that sells. They should consider providing personal notes that are handcrafted for a small office rather than the typical pitches provided by traditional advertisers. Email messages should be kept very short. Internet users may receive hundreds of messages per day online. It is helpful to come up with a three or four word subject line that summarizes your advertisement. Sometimes incentive sales, such as providing cash for sales or entries in drawings for prizes, will be helpful in attracting attention to clicking onto your advertisement. Incentive sites are available on the internet to help in this process through outsourcing. Discounts, free samples, and limited time offers are also helpful to get persons to buy on the internet.

The use of the new social media such as Twitter, Facebook and You Tube, are also important to marketing on the internet and to marketing in general today. The traditional media often can be bypassed to reach out over the internet by using the new social media to directly reach many persons. Marketers can use these new media to communicate directly at any time to many persons interested in the company and what products and services it offers. The internet and the new social media permit rapid feedback to the firm from the public. The internet can help firms engage in new conversations that are not readily available from the traditional media. These conversations may help the firm increase web traffic and sales for the firm.

Online customers may be very different from customers that have been reached by more traditional media such as newspapers and television. Google today already has more advertising revenue than al the major television networks combined. New advertising media on the internet such as craigslist have provided options to advertisers that may replace or reinforce traditional classified advertising in print medial such as newspapers or magazines.

One advantage in utilizing the internet and the new social media is that communication can be two ways. This may permit a marketer at a firm to reach out to possible customers and other stakeholders and quickly learn whether its ideas and products are feasible or need to be retooled to achieve success in the market place.

Search engines can be used to help develop better placement, ranking of sites and other positioning on the internet. Online advertising, buying ads and use of advertising auctions can be developed. Affiliate programs with pay per click, pay per lead and similar promotions can make advertising more effective in some situations.

Today there are many internet companies that specialize in internet advertising. These companies are often willing to pay website publishers on a cost per impression or on a cost per click basis. Internet advertising rates tend to be low, and sites with inventory can often add extra income through participation. These internet advertising specialists can offer a low cost advertising channel compared with direct site advertising purchases.

www.SmallBizManager.com offers a number of marketing focused resources to help the marketer find strategies and specific tactics for business marketing and sales on the internet. Their section on Web Marketing offers an excellent resource with a wealth of articles, research and links. Their Idea Site offers a useful marketing and sales site "for creative business people" geared to home-based and smaller businesses. Some other subject areas on www.SmallBizManager.com offers sales focused resources such as selling information, training to lead generation and hiring, as well as sales psychology that works, how to select a sales force that sells, best techniques, and the pros and cons of co-branding.

There are also many community resources to help in the internet marketing process. Online magazines, trade shows, professional associations, industry news, and company research directories are useful community resources. There are government resources such as statistics, grants, funding sources, and information on regulations that can be helpful also in this process. Local public libraries and libraries at colleges and universities also provide much useful reference information on what is available on the internet.

There are many new digital tools that can be used to develop name recognition and sales for the firm.

Podcasting is a method that is similar to a radio or television broadcast without the restriction to a specific time slot that is required by a radio or television broadcast. Podcasting is a personal broadcast online that can be downloaded in digital audio or in a video format to a computer, iPod, iPhone, Blackberry or MP3 player. Podcasts can be used to enable visitors to a company's web site to learn about the company's products and services or to see specific items such as marketing programs, advertising, and speeches by company executives. Without paying for advertising on radio, television, or print media a company can use podcasting to reach an audience all over the world through downloading from the internet. Podcasting enables a prospective customer to be able to view or listen to the message of the company at a time and place convenient to the prospective customer.

A blog is a website developed by either an individual or a company or other organization for the purpose of posting information on the web site for others to comment or give their reactions. Blogging can enable a company to quickly get out information on its new products and services. Potential customers can react speedily to the blog enabling the company to understand the view of these potential customers. The blog can then be revised to provide more information, reinforce the message of the company on its products and services or provide revised information or revised products and services in reaction to comments made regarding the blog. Blogs can help a company spread information and can help a company increase its reputation by speedy reaction to comments of potential customers.

A wiki is another type of web site that anyone can offer to update or revise such as the Wikipedia Encyclopedia. Some wikis are revised by anyone without checking on the reliability of the update or revision, while others maintain controls over how the website is revised or updated to try to make sure that the proposed updating or revision is credible. While all wikis may not be credible, a company needs to review wikis that comment on the company to make sure that the wiki is accurate and does not provide false information on the company.

As mentioned above, social networking such as Twitter or Facebook is another new tool that must be considered by every marketer today. Social networking allows persons on the network to converse with each other on topics of mutual interest and to invite their friends to be part of a web-based community. Ideas and information can be shared on these social networks. These social networks can help companies distribute information and ideas to persons who may spread this information quickly to many persons. Many of these social networks appeal to young persons who wish to communicate with each other on many ideas and concepts. Some social networks are being developed for persons of more diverse ages that have something in common. For example, LinkedIn is a social network for persons interested in careers.

You Tube and other similar services provide short videos of popular downloads from the internet. Anyone can make a video and can post it on You Tube for the world to see. Organizations can use You Tube to bring short videos to wide-spread attention. Even charitable organizations have used You Tube to popularize their charities. For example, the St. Baldrick's Foundation raises funds for research to fight cancer in children by encouraging their supporters to raise funds for the foundation by holding events where persons volunteer to have their heads shaved for donations to the foundation by friends of the persons who have volunteered to have their heads shaved. Publicity for these events through You Tube videos of having persons having their heads shaved to benefit the charity has increased the visibility of the foundation and has enabled the foundation to receive additional funds in donations for use in trying to find a cure for cancer in children. You Tube and similar online services can help a company get better known if it can develop creative videos that persons interested in the company's products and services can watch online.

Think of traditional marketing as your company's identity. Traditional marketing media includes all direct and indirect advertising and other medial that your company should use to get your message out day by day. Think of social media as the voice and identity (message) of your prospects and existing customers.

Social media can be used by your company to be able to have an impact on prospective customers of your company that allows for a free flowing conversation between you and your customers. Social media provide ways to feel and understand the opinions of your present and prospective customers over a period of time.

The following is a checklist of some ideas that marketers can use to help their companies succeed:

1. Start a fan page for customers who are pleased with the products and services of your company. Let these customers become fans of your company

112

on Facebook. This can serve as a central hub of your company's social media activity.

2.   Develop applications that will use social media sites to tap into social media users on behalf of your company.

3.   Keep content on your website updated. People who see that you keep your site current will check out your site again and again.

4.   Listen and analyze what your customers and potential customers say about your company and its products and services. Respond to comments and concerns about your organization and its services online just as you might respond to similar comments received in person or over the telephone.

5.   Try to have useful conversations with members of your social media network and community. This will help develop loyalty to your company by persons you have contacted through social media.

6.   Set up an upcoming events section on your social media. This will help persons learn what is going on and will help you generate more interest in your events.

7.   Use a variety of social media platforms. Depending on your audience, it might be helpful for you to expand use of social medial beyond any one platform as different platforms may appeal to different persons.

8.   Monitor your social medial platforms every day so as to be aware of what is happening and to enable a response as quickly as possible.

9.   Use social media to help build your brand. Make sure that your social media is consistent in colors, logos and styles with other media that you use.

This checklist has been adapted from an article by Andy Kelley, CEO of Effective Student Marketing, Inc. as published in *Career Education Review*, March 2010.

Social media such as Twitter, Facebook and You Tube can also help develop awareness of the company and its products and services by enabling the firm to target specific groups that may be interested in the firm's services or products.

Another new concept is developing a virtual realty world. Virtual reality worlds can provide opportunities for companies to get their products and services used by some of the virtual characters in a virtual reality community. One of these virtual reality communities already has more than one million participants. Participation in a virtual reality community may be another opportunity for a new company to get known quickly.

Use of the internet and other new media such as the new social media changes quickly. The marketing executive needs to take advantage of the internet and the new medial to better develop marketing in his or her organization.

INDEX

www.ingramcontent.com/pod-product-compliance
Lightning Source LLC
Chambersburg PA
CBHW061336220326
41599CB00026B/5211